JOHN ADAMS AND THE FEAR OF
AMERICAN OLIGARCHY

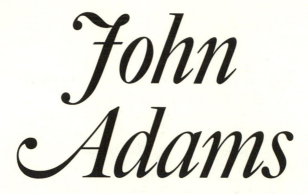

John Adams

AND THE FEAR OF

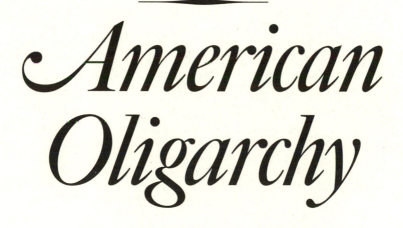

American Oligarchy

LUKE MAYVILLE

PRINCETON UNIVERSITY PRESS
Princeton & Oxford

PUBLISHED BY PRINCETON UNIVERSITY PRESS,
41 William Street, Princeton, New Jersey 08540

IN THE UNITED KINGDOM: PRINCETON UNIVERSITY PRESS,
6 Oxford Street, Woodstock, Oxfordshire OX20 1TR

press.princeton.edu

The quotation on page v is copyright © 2014 by Garry Wills and was first published in the *New York Review of Books*.

Frontispiece and cover art from The New York Public Library. Miriam and Ira D. Wallach Division of Art, Prints and Photographs: Print Collection, The New York Public Library. "John Adams," New York Public Library Digital Collections. Accessed June 13, 2016. http://digitalcollections.nypl.org /items/510d47da-2fd6-a3d9-e040-e00a18064a99

First paperback printing, 2019

Paper ISBN: 978-0-691-18324-4

The Library of Congress has cataloged the cloth edition as follows:

Names: Mayville, Luke, 1985– author.
Title: John Adams and the fear of American oligarchy / Luke Mayville.
Description: Princeton : Princeton University Press, 2016. | Includes bibliographical references and index.
Identifiers: LCCN 2016003613 | ISBN 9780691171531 (hardcover : alk. paper)
Subjects: LCSH: Adams, John, 1735–1826—Political and social views. | United States—Politics and government—1783–1809. | United States—Politics and government—1775–1783. | Oligarchy—United States.
Classification: LCC E322 .M36 2016 | DDC 973.4/4092—dc23 LC record available at http://lccn.loc.gov/2016003613

British Library Cataloging-in-Publication Data is available

This book has been composed in Adobe Caslon Pro

Printed on acid-free paper. ∞

TO MY MOTHER

The proof that we live in a plutocracy is not that the wealthy get most of the prizes in our society, but that majorities think that is how it should be.

—GARRY WILLS, *New York Review of Books*, January 2014

Or do you suppose that the regimes arise "from an oak or rocks" and not from the dispositions of the men in the cities, which, tipping the scale as it were, draw the rest along with them?

—SOCRATES, in Plato's *Republic*

The Distinction of property will have more influence than all the rest in commercial countries, if it is not rivalled by some other distinction.

—JOHN ADAMS, notes on Mary Wollstonecraft's *Historical and Moral View of the Origin and Progress of the French Revolution*

Contents

Acknowledgments

THIS BOOK WAS MADE possible by the generous support of many individuals and institutions. I am especially indebted to the Yale University Department of Political Science, where I wrote the doctoral dissertation from which this project was adapted. I must first acknowledge my dissertation committee. Special thanks to Steven Smith, who accepted me as a student for no good reason and who patiently ushered this project from a four-page proposal to its current form. I am also deeply indebted to Bryan Garsten, who challenged me to think *with* historical texts and not just about them, and who first suggested that my thoughts were worthy of book form. Thanks also to Karuna Mantena, whose advice was indispensable at moments when my project lost focus. Stephen Skowronek, David Mayhew, and Andrew Sabl read much or all of the manuscript and provided helpful advice for revision. Other Yale faculty who supported the project or gave advice include Ian Shapiro, Danilo Petranovich, and Helene Landemore. Many of my fellow graduate students also shaped this project directly or indirectly, including Lucas Thompson, David Lebow, Shawn Fraistat, Joshua Braver, Teresa Bejan, Lucas Entel, Travis Pantin, Celia Paris, Blake Emerson, Anurag Sinha, Matt Longo, Andrea Katz, Adom Getachew, Peter Verovsek, Navid Hassanpour, Lisa Gilson, Robert Arnold, Lionel Beehner, Stefan Eich, Umur Basdas, Brandon Terry, and Josh Simon. Other scholars who supported this project were Joshua Cherniss, Prithvi Datta, Michael Lamb, Jim Wilson, Loubna El Amine, Jeffrey Green, John McCormick, Nadia Urbinati, Melissa Lane, Aziz Rana, Benjamin Ewing, Lisa Herzog, Daren Staloff, Michael Zuckert, David Grewal, Patrick Weil, Madhav Khosla, Aurelian Craiutu,

Pratap Bhanu Mehta, and Jeffry Burnam. Special thanks to James Read and Alex Zakaras for reading entire chapters at a critical stage and providing invaluable comments.

I am deeply indebted to Danielle Allen, who provided me with a model of civic-minded scholarship and who encouraged this project at a moment when its prospects were uncertain. I am also very grateful for several conversations with Joseph J. Ellis, who encouraged me to reach an audience beyond the academy and who paved the way for this book with his own scholarship on the theme of inequality in John Adams's writings.

I am grateful to the Jack Miller Center and the Yale Center for the Study of Representative Institutions for creating an intellectual environment in which the study of American political thought can thrive. I also owe a great debt of gratitude to the Political Theory Institute at American University, where I worked on this project as a postdoctoral fellow for the year 2014–2015. While at AU, I had the privilege of teaching two seminars, "American Political Thought" and "Inequality and Democracy," both of which helped sharpen the concepts and arguments found in these pages. I would like to thank the students of these seminars and also the many AU faculty who supported my work, including Alan Levine, Thomas Merrill, Jeremy Janow, and Sarah Houser. The final stage of production was carried out with the support of Columbia University and the Columbia Center for American Studies, where I currently reside as a postdoctoral fellow. Special thanks are due to Casey Blake, Andrew Delbanco, Tamara Mann Tweel, Angela Darling, Roosevelt Montás, and the unforgettable students in my 2015–2016 section of Contemporary Civilization.

I owe a special thanks to Rob Tempio, Gail Schmitt, Debbie Tegarden, Ryan Mulligan, Chris Ferrante, Doreen Perry, Jaime Estrada, and everyone else at Princeton University Press who helped produce this book. Thank you to Nancy Gerth, my fellow

Idahoan, for her careful indexing work. Thanks also to the editorial staff at *Polity* and to anonymous reviewers who shaped and supported my first published work on the political theory of John Adams.

I have been fortunate to share versions of the chapters that follow with many workshops and conferences, and I owe many thanks to the Georgetown Political Theory Workshop, the Yale Political Theory Workshop, the Penn Graduate Political Theory Workshop, the Princeton Graduate Conference in Political Theory, the Rothermere American Institute, the Association for Political Theory, the Northeastern Political Science Association Annual Conference, the New England Political Science Annual Conference, and the American Political Science Association Annual Conference.

This book is a first for me, and so I would like to thank all of the teachers and mentors who encouraged me to think and write. Special thanks to Jackie Hanna, Marianne Love, George Marker, Woody Aunan, Lou Goodness, Julie and Kim Keaton, Christa and Frank Faucett, Janet Whitney, Kerrie Trotter Henson, Dennis Gilbert, Lynn Tullis, Michelle Lippert, Jane Cramer, Craig Parsons, Gail Unruh, and Ken DeBevoise.

To my wife, Elena, for her love and her edits, I express my deepest gratitude. I am also grateful for the support of my brother, Johnny, and for ongoing encouragement from Brian, Marguerite, Matthew, Davern, Nicole, Rick, and Father John P. Duffell. Finally, I dedicate this work to my mother, for nurturing my curiosity and for so much more.

JOHN ADAMS AND THE FEAR OF
AMERICAN OLIGARCHY

Introduction

O N A COLD DECEMBER night in 1786, barricaded behind stacks of books in his library in London's Grosvenor Square, John Adams made the fateful decision to begin writing. The mere act of putting pen to paper racked his nerves. "The manual exercise of writing," he later recalled, "was painful and distressing to me, almost like a blow on the elbow or the knee."[1] For it was not just any writing project. It was the first of his public efforts to criticize the democratic revolution.

The final outcome of this project would be two works. The first, the three-volume *Defence of the Constitutions of Government of the United States of America*, would eventually be hailed as "the finest fruit of the American enlightenment."[2] The second work, entitled *Discourses on Davila*, would earn Adams recognition as "the most assiduous American student of 'social psychology' in the eighteenth century."[3]

What made the undertaking so distressing was the knowledge that he was in some ways turning against the democratic movement he had done so much to build. Almost no one had championed the revolutionary cause as vigorously as had John Adams. Now, at the very moment when the revolution that had begun in America was sweeping the Atlantic world, Adams was deciding to convert from catalyst to critic. In the process, he worried, he would make enemies of "the French patriots, the Dutch patriots, the English republicans, dissenters, reformers." And most worrisome of all, he lamented: "What came nearer home to my bosom than all the rest, I knew I should give offence to many, if not all, of my best friends in America."[4]

This worry would turn out to be well justified. The two major works of political theory that would grow out of his critical efforts would contribute greatly to the widespread belief that Adams had abandoned his republican origins. "In truth," Adams would later lament to Jefferson, "my 'Defence of the Constitutions' and 'Discourses on Davila,' were the cause of that immense unpopularity which fell like the tower of Siloam upon me."[5] The common narrative, which would be propagated by his critics and would be picked up and repeated by later generations, was that Adams, the erstwhile revolutionary, had undergone a fundamental change of mind during his sojourn as a diplomat in Europe. As Jefferson would write, Adams had been seduced in Europe by the "glare of royalty and nobility."[6] And at the same time, the story would go, he had been overcome by reactionary dread upon learning of Shays' Rebellion and other popular disturbances back in America. Adams's *Defence* and *Discourses*, both of which casually discussed the role of aristocracy in America and seemed sympathetic to monarchical forms of government, were interpreted to be the clearest evidence that Adams had indeed betrayed his early republican convictions.

Perhaps what pained Adams most at the outset of his critical turn was the likelihood that he would be deeply misunderstood. As he would insist repeatedly in the decades that followed, he never intended to call for inegalitarian institutions. "I will forfeit my life," he offered Jefferson, "if you can find one sentiment in my Defence of the Constitutions, or the Discourses on Davila, which, by a fair construction, can favor the introduction of hereditary monarchy or aristocracy into America."[7]

If indeed Adams's decision to criticize the democratic revolution was evidence of a turn to aristocratic sympathies, such a turn would have represented an abrupt departure from his humble origins. Born and raised in the quiet agricultural village of Braintree, Massachusetts, he descended from a line of middling farmers and artisans going back to his great-great-grandfather

Henry, a malter and farmer who first settled the Adams family in New England in 1636. A glimpse of the future statesman could be seen in Henry's great-grandson and John Adams's father, the elder John Adams, who served the Braintree community as a deacon of the church, a lieutenant in the local militia, and a selectman in the town meeting. Still, by occupation the elder John Adams was a shoemaker and farmer, a plain Puritan whose ambition hardly reached beyond his aspiration to see his eldest son attend Harvard College and join the clergy. The young John Adams would spurn his father's wish and enter the legal profession, choosing public life over the pulpit. But he never forsook his identity as a simple New England farmer. Indeed, even long after he acquired great fame, he never acquired a sizable fortune, and he continued until his last days to consider himself a middling farmer. Strange indeed was the label "aristocrat" to describe a man who, even while serving as the nation's first vice president, continued to self-identify as a plebeian.[8]

Even stranger was the label of "aristocrat" when considered alongside Adams's credentials as a leader of the revolution. In the year 1765, at twenty-nine years old, he had published *A Dissertation on the Canon and Feudal Law*, a fiery tract that laid out his view of the emergence of freedom in the American colonies and the dangers posed to that freedom by reactionary forces. A decade later, amid mounting grievances against parliamentary overreach, Adams penned a sharp critique of British imperial policy in the form of a series of papers published under the pseudonym Novanglus. In the spring of 1776, when the various colonies began plans to revolutionize their governments and draw up new state constitutions, it was to Adams they turned for ideas on the principles and institutions of republican government. Adams's *Thoughts on Government*, originally written as a letter to his fellow revolutionary Richard Henry Lee of Virginia,

was widely circulated in the colonies and became the blueprint for several state constitutions. It was no surprise that in
1779, when it came time to frame a constitution for the state of
Massachusetts, it was Adams who was called upon as the chief
draftsman.[9]

Adams's revolutionary agitation was not limited to the written word. Thomas Jefferson, to whom Adams had delegated the
task of drafting a declaration of independence, would later recollect that it was Adams who championed the declaration in
speech. Though sometimes lacking in grace and elegance, Adams
was nonetheless "our colossus on the floor," at times speaking
with a "power of thought and expression" that "moved us from
our seats."[10] Furthermore, Adams was among the cause's chief
behind-the-scenes agitators.[11] Utterly committed to furthering
the revolutionary cause through strategic action, Adams orches-
trated the committee to draft the Declaration of Independence,
plotted to appoint George Washington head of the Continental
army, and, when later deployed as a diplomat in Europe, played
an integral role in negotiating peace with Great Britain and securing loans from Dutch financiers.

Could it be that a man so devoted to the revolutionary cause
suddenly betrayed his conviction and embraced the aristocratic
forms of the old world? As we will see, it was a grave misun-
derstanding to construe Adams as an apologist for aristocracy.
Just as Adams the politician had been wholly committed to the
republican revolution, Adams the writer and thinker had long
been committed to articulating and defending the foundational
principles of republican self-government. His critical turn came
not from a change of disposition, but from the conviction that
his fellow revolutionaries had substituted ideology for sober analysis, that they had disregarded essential facts of political life, and
that in doing so they had jeopardized the republican experiment
that he had done so much to initiate.

From a young age Adams had engaged deeply in what could be called practical political science. As a lawyer-in-training, he had studied historical political constitutions alongside the writings of political philosophers in an effort to illuminate the principles of republican order. In a diary entry written at the age of twenty-three, he spelled out the ambition of his studies:

> Keep your law book or some point of law in your mind, at least, six hours in a day. . . . Labor to get distinct ideas of law, right, wrong, justice, equity . . . aim at an exact knowledge of the nature, end, and means of government; compare the different forms of it with each other, and each of them with their effects on public and private happiness. Study Seneca, Cicero, and all other good moral Writers. Study Montesquieu, Bolingbroke . . . and all other good, civil Writers.[12]

This commitment and resolve would not weaken with age. By the 1780s Adams had come to view the study of politics and government as a duty owed to future generations. "I must study politics and war," Adams famously wrote,

> that my sons may have liberty to study mathematics and philosophy. My sons ought to study mathematics and philosophy, geography, natural history and naval architecture, navigation, commerce and agriculture, in order to give their children a right to study painting, poetry, music, architecture, statuary, tapestry and porcelain.[13]

Living at a time when the United States was widely viewed as a precarious experiment, Adams believed that the study of politics was integral to human flourishing. Thus, even as he rose to public eminence, he would never abandon his vocation as a political scientist.

Adams's fateful decision to write *Defence of the Constitutions* was motivated by the belief that the principles he had done so much to institutionalize were now being profoundly misunderstood. At the heart of the matter, from Adams's perspective, was a profound naiveté about the power of social and economic elites. For the likes of Thomas Paine, Thomas Jefferson, and other leading lights of the age of revolution, there was an assumption that the power of wealth and family name was a vestige of the Old World, an artificial feature of monarchy and aristocracy that would disappear once those forms were abolished. What the ideologues of revolution had failed to understand was that the power of privilege was so deeply rooted that it would persist even in modern democratic republics.

Adams's critique was not single-mindedly focused on the power of elites. Like many of his Founding Era contemporaries, Adams feared that the popular energies unleashed by the revolution might result in tyrannical majorities and the undermining of property rights and the rule of law. Indeed, near the end of his life, at the Massachusetts Convention of 1820, Adams took an infamous stand against the expansion of the suffrage beyond property holders, citing a fear that the propertyless, if granted the right to vote, would "vote us out of our houses."[14] A similar anxiety appeared in the third volume of the *Defence*, in which Adams predicted that the majority, if given absolute power, would abolish all debt and would plunder the rich through taxes and expropriation. "The idle, the vicious, and the intemperate," meanwhile, "would rush into the utmost extravagance of debauchery."[15] Long before the *Defence*, even as he agitated for the patriot cause in the years preceding the revolution, he harbored a commitment to the rule of law that frequently put him at odds with his compatriots. This was especially the case in the spring of 1770, when British troops fired on a group of patriot agitators, leaving eight wounded and three dead. While leaders of the patriot movement demanded vengeance for what came to be called the Boston Massacre, Adams's commitment to impartiality led him to rush to the side of the perpetrators and to sign on as their defense lawyer.[16]

And yet, for all of his worries about the rule of law and the unruly many, Adams's chief preoccupation was with the danger posed by the wealthy and wellborn few. This preoccupation was evident as early as his *Dissertation on the Canon and Feudal Law*, in which the twenty-nine-year-old railed against a pernicious class of men descended from "high churchmen and high statesman." The New England political order, argued Adams, had been built upon an explicit rejection of rule by an oligarchic elite. Through prolonged struggle, New Englanders had eliminated all homage, duties, and services paid to lords by landholders, and they had successfully replaced the priestly class of the Old World with an ordination process based only on "the foundation of the Bible and common sense." Perhaps most important, they had thrown off the yoke of ignorance by diffusing knowledge such that "the education of all ranks of people was made the care and expense of the public in a manner that I believe has been unknown to any other people ancient or modern."[17] Yet now, Adams observed, a new class of elites had set out to effect "an entire subversion of the whole system of our fathers by the introduction of the canon and feudal systems in America."[18] The emerging oligarchy had sought, among other things, to censure the public provision of education as "a needless expense and an imposition upon the rich in favor of the poor and as an institution productive of idleness and vain speculation among the people."[19] The class of men he referred to in the *Dissertation* as grandees would change considerably during his lifetime: from the would-be feudal lords of the mid-eighteenth century to the commercial elite of the early nineteenth century. What would not change, as we will see, was

Adams's preoccupation with elite power and the danger it posed to republican institutions.

When the retired, elderly Adams reflected on his political writings, he described aristocracy as a major theme. Recalling his decision that night in London to set his critical sights on the revolution, he described his choice explicitly as a resolution to write something on the neglected subject of aristocracy.[20] Adams insisted that aristocrats had not disappeared from modern republics. They continued to be, as they always had been, "the most difficult animals to manage of any thing in the whole theory and practice of government." In spite of the abolition of formal titles of nobility, there remained a class of men in America and in all republics who "will not suffer themselves to be governed," men who "not only exert all their own subtlety, industry, and courage, but they employ the commonalty to knock to pieces every plan and model that the most honest architects in legislation can invent to keep them within bounds."[21] As we will see, Adams set out to criticize the democratic revolution not from an attachment to aristocrats but from a fear of them.

Indeed, it is most accurate to say that Adams's writings were motivated by a fear of *oligarchy*. For when Adams obsessively wrote of aristocrats, he was not referring to that group of men whom the ancient Greeks had labeled the *aristoi*, meaning "the best." What Adams had in mind was those whom the likes of Plato and Aristotle had called oligarchs—those distinguished primarily not by merit but by such qualities as family name, beauty, and especially wealth. This class was designated as "the few" (*hoi oligoi*), a class standing apart from the "the many" (*hoi polloi*). Thinkers in the Western tradition had varied widely in their moral evaluations of the few, but many shared the view that oligarchic power was a stable, constitutive feature of republican politics. Insofar as republican governments were successful, their success was due in part to institutions and practices that successfully managed or counterbalanced oligarchic power.[22]

What Adams feared was that modern republics would fail in this regard. He adhered firmly to the classical tradition even as his contemporaries began to conceive of society not as divided among the few and the many but instead as consisting of a single, unified populace. As we will see, Adams believed that this new class-blind mode of conceiving of a democratic-republican society entailed a dangerous neglect of the problem of oligarchic power.[23]

Though Adams's contemporaries, along with many intellectual historians of later years, took his obsession with aristocracy as evidence of an intention to defend class privilege, much closer to the mark was the interpretation of C. Wright Mills, the renowned sociologist and author of *The Power Elite*. Contemplating the powerful political-economic elite of twentieth-century America, Mills found in Adams's writings a precursor to his own analysis. Likewise, political theorist Judith Shklar identified Adams not as an aristocrat apologist but as the progenitor of a long American tradition of decrying and criticizing elite domination.[24] Indeed, as we will see, when Adams harangued his contemporaries on the topic of aristocracy, his intention was not to justify elite power but to criticize it, and especially to resist the democratic temptation to wish away elite power and in the process to leave it unregulated.

READING ADAMS

This book presents John Adams as a student and critic of the political power of elites. This characterization will surprise some scholars familiar with his writings. Just as Adams's contemporaries often viewed him as an apologist for aristocracy, historians have frequently interpreted him as a defender of oligarchy rather than as a critic of it. Joyce Appleby has written that by the time Adams wrote his mature political works, he had "reassessed the political affirmations he had formed as a revolutionary leader" and had embraced the conservatism of many European *Anglomanes*— those who admired and wished to replicate the English constitution and its balance of power between the king, House of Lords, and House of Commons. In practical terms, this meant welcoming in America "institutions giving permanent political power to an assigned group."[25] Likewise, an older line of interpretation considered Adams to be a founding father of American conservatism. Russell Kirk, who famously appropriated the thought of Edmund Burke as the foundation for the modern conservative disposition, found in John Adams a like-minded American figure. According to Kirk, Adams shared nearly all of Burke's basic commitments:

> Both declare the necessity of religious belief to sustain society, both exalt practical considerations above abstract theory, both contrast man's imperfect real nature with the fantastic claims of the *philosophes*, both stand for a balanced government which recognizes the natural distinctions of man from man, class from class, interest from interest.[26]

Much like Appleby, though with different purposes in mind, Kirk viewed Adams as a conservative apologist for class privilege—a characterization difficult to square with the one found in these pages.

A number of important studies of Adams's political thought have convincingly recovered him from the camp of reactionary conservatism but have nonetheless overlooked the centrality of the theme of oligarchy in his political writings. One school of thought, inspired in part by Hannah Arendt's treatment of

Adams in her *On Revolution*, has presented him as a propo-
nent of a "classical republican" tradition beginning in ancient
Greece and reaching its demise with the rise of modern commercialism. On this account, John Adams stands as an American exemplar of a long line of thinkers who understood that
"public freedom consisted in having a share in public business,
and that the activities connected with this business by no means
constituted a burden but gave those who discharged them in
public a feeling of happiness they could acquire nowhere else."
Likewise, J.G.A. Pocock has similarly called Adams's *Defence
of the Constitutions* "perhaps the last major work of political
theory written within the unmodified tradition of classical
republicanism."[27]

Meanwhile, whereas the classical republican reading has presented Adams as centrally concerned with public virtue, a line of
interpretation that we might call classical liberal has drawn him
as a constitutionalist focused on the securing of natural rights
by means of elaborate political architecture. C. Bradley Thompson's *John Adams and the Spirit of Liberty*—the most thorough
and comprehensive study of Adams's political thought to date—
has presented Adams as above all a practical political scientist
who, like James Madison and the other leading framers of the
US Constitution, understood that the security of natural rights
depended on a complex of institutions capable of controlling and
elevating man's passions and interests. Thompson has registered
many of the themes explored in this book. He has noted that "no
subject interested Adams more than the nature and origins of
human inequality" and that one of the main goals of his institutional design was the containment of aristocratic ambition.[28] But
Thompson's presentation of Adams as a classical-liberal constitutionalist, much like classical-republican readings, have neglected
the central importance of Adams's thoroughgoing critique of oligarchic power. Though these studies effectively rescued Adams

from the charge of reactionary conservatism, they did not give pride of place to his preoccupation with the politics of inequality.

The seeds of the perspective of this book are found in Gordon Wood's stand-alone chapter on John Adams in his *Creation of the American Republic*. To a certain extent Wood read Adams much as Appleby would a few years later—as an outmoded and reactionary thinker attached to Old World institutions and incapable of comprehending the political innovations of his time. Yet even as Wood presented Adams as antiquated and "irrelevant" in the ideological context of the early republic, he also presented him as an anomalous figure harboring a preoccupation with matters of inequality and oligarchy at a time when his peers were inventing a liberal ideology that obscured these matters. "For too long and with too much candor," wrote Wood, "he had tried to tell his fellow Americans some truths about themselves that American values and American ideology would not admit."[29] Wood left vague what these truths were. This book aims to clarify at least one of them.

A few studies have explicitly recognized Adams as a biting critic of oligarchic power. In his classic comparative study of the late-eighteenth-century revolutions of the Atlantic world, R. R. Palmer recognized that even though Adams was often called an aristocrat, it was always clear from his writings that "aristocracy was Adams's principal bugaboo."[30] Judith Shklar similarly characterized Adams as preoccupied with the dangers posed by aristocracy. Writing of the "suspicion of aristocracy" that has appeared again and again in the American political tradition, Shklar wrote that "no figure in the early history of the Republic mirrored and thought through these attitudes more urgently or intensely than did John Adams." The various diatribes against elite power by later Americans, from Thorsten Veblen's critique of elite behavior to the progressive "denunciation of corruption" to the populist "outcry against monopolized power," all echoed Adams.[31]

If these last references provide useful hints about Adams's preoccupation with social and economic elites, several works of biography have more directly anticipated my study by recognizing and elaborating the theme of oligarchy in Adams's political thought. Joseph Ellis has found that for Adams the "central dilemma of political science" was that of controlling the energies of elite factions. Adams was immune, Ellis has written, "to the seductive illusions that had established themselves as central assumptions in post-revolutionary political culture." The point Adams was at pains to make, noted Ellis, was that "in all societies for which there was any kind of historical record, political power and wealth tended to go hand in hand; and a few people invariably accumulated more wealth and power than the others."[32] Likewise, according to John Ferling it was the growing sway of financiers, speculators, and merchants that motivated Adams eventually to abandon the Federalist Party. "It was humanity's oppression at the hands of the wealthy few," Ferling observed, "that Adams thought most likely, and it was that which he most dreaded."[33] John Patrick Diggins similarly presented Adams as an antidote to Jefferson, Paine, and others who "championed the French Revolution as the death of monarchy and had no qualms about the new life of money." Adams has been called an aristocrat defending wealth, argued Diggins, "when he was actually a moralist admonishing it." A defender of executive power and critic of the rich, Adams foreshadowed Theodore Roosevelt's progressive effort to assert the might of the presidency against the "malefactors of wealth."[34]

Yet if scholars have noticed Adams as an early student of wealth and politics, they have stopped short of revealing his critique of oligarchic power in all of its depth. As we will see, what makes Adams's writings relevant today is not just that he shared our concerns with inequality and the threat of oligarchy, but that he analyzed these features of political life with striking originality. Adams's writings uniquely synthesized two patterns of thought. The first was a mode of inquiry that we might call practical political science: a lifelong study of political institutions informed by experience and guided by historians and political philosophers from Plato to Polybius, from Machiavelli to Montesquieu. The second was the late-eighteenth-century Scottish Enlightenment, an intellectual movement preoccupied with the moral-psychological dynamics of the emerging commercial order. It was a synthesis of these two strains of thought—practical political science and Scottish moral psychology—that led Adams to understand the power of wealth as rooted in the human psyche.

WEALTH AND POWER

What can John Adams teach us about wealth and power in our own times? I wish to suggest that he can help us as we attempt to comprehend and respond to one of today's most urgent problems: the outsized influence of wealth in our politics. We have learned in recent years that, in spite of the widespread democratic expectation that the decisions of elected officials should reflect the preferences of ordinary citizens, the decisions of policy makers all too often reflect the preferences of the affluent and, even more so, the superrich.[35] How is it that a wealthy minority wields such influence in a political system expected to empower majorities? If there is a single prevailing theory today about how the rich get their way in politics, it is that they are able to *buy* political influence. The rich purchase electoral voice through campaign contributions and powerful opinion-shaping institutions. They win in Washington with deep-pocketed lobbying efforts and what Jeffrey Winters has called an "income defense industry" consisting of lawyers, accountants, and wealth-management consultants.[36] Yet in today's context, this explanation appears insufficient. Can the lobbying efforts of Bill Gates and Mark Zuckerberg account for the enormous influence of their views on issues ranging from education to immigration policy? Can the appeal of billionaire candidates like Donald Trump be measured merely with reference to their campaign spending? Wealth, it seems, enjoys even greater influence than it is able to buy.

In the course of his political writings, Adams elaborated an understanding of the power of wealth that might aid us in our quandary. If today's students of money and politics have understood the power of wealth largely in terms of purchasing power—a power to bankroll campaigns, purchase media space, and fund lobbying efforts—Adams traced the political influence of wealth not just to its power to buy but to its grip on the human mind. Though he was no stranger to the purchase of political influence, Adams repeatedly urged his readers to appreciate sentiments like sympathy and admiration for wealth as less tangible but no less potent sources of oligarchic power.

In his letters, essays, and treatises, Adams explored in subtle detail what might be called *soft* oligarchy—the disproportionate power that accrues to wealth on account of widespread sympathy for the rich. As scholars of international relations have long known, coercion through the use of brute force and inducement through monetary payment are not the only available forms of power. In addition to the powers of compensation and coercion—carrots and sticks—there is also "soft" power, defined by Joseph Nye as "the ability to get what you want through attraction rather than coercion or payments." The United States, for example, wields soft power when the world's people admire its ideals and are attracted to its culture. Favorable sentiments, rather than carrots and sticks, lead populations around the world to want what the United States wants and to follow it willingly.[37] It was something like this type of soft empire that John Adams attributed to wealth. The power of riches was not only the ability to coerce through relations of material dependency or to induce through direct payments, but also the ability to command influence through sentiments like admiration and sympathy.

Similar to the way the subjects of monarchies had admired royalty and nobility, the citizens of commercial republics would tend to admire the rich. In commercial society the people tended to associate wealth with happiness and therefore to look up to and celebrate the wealthiest citizens as the happiest. Adams drew on the moral psychology of Adam Smith to describe how public admiration of wealth, much like public admiration of royalty, could be a potent source of political power. In *The Theory of Moral Sentiments* Smith had described the "disposition of mankind . . . to go along with all the passions of the rich and the powerful" and the obsequiousness to our superiors that "arises from our admiration for the advantages of their situation." "We are eager," Smith wrote, "to assist them in completing a system of happiness that approaches so near to perfection; and we desire to serve them for their own sake, without any other recompense but the vanity or the honor of obliging them."[38]

John Adams's innovation was to apply this lesson of moral psychology to the political realm. The political power of wealth, he insisted, could not be fully appreciated without understanding its roots in public sentiments. Though it was true that oligarchic power derived in large part from more tangible sources, such as social connections and relations of material dependency, Adams insisted that "there is a degree of admiration, abstracted from all dependence, obligation, expectation, or even acquaintance, which accompanies splendid wealth, insures some respect, and bestows some influence."[39] Adams did not deny the importance of the purchase of political influence by money. It was "a natural and unchangeable inconvenience in all popular elections," he wrote in *Defence of the Constitutions of Government of the United States*, "that he who has the deepest purse, or the fewest scruples about using it, will generally prevail."[40] But Adams also traced the influence of wealth to the deep admiration for the rich felt by the public and to the insatiable appetite for that same admiration possessed by society's most ambitious. It was the *grandeur* of wealth, and not merely its purchasing power, that accounted for its immense political influence.

Political theorists have paid ample attention to the corrupting influence of wealth but have largely neglected the sentiments of the public as a source of oligarchic power. John Rawls argued that the outsized influence of the rich on the political process undermines the basic principle that all citizens, regardless of social or economic position, must possess "a fair opportunity to hold public office and to influence the outcome of political decisions."[41] Similarly, Michael Walzer has influentially contended that the disproportionate political influence of wealth undermines the foundations of liberalism by allowing one's standing in one sphere of life to dictate one's position in another.[42] Just as liberalism requires protecting the sphere of civil society from that of state power, argued Walzer, it is also necessary to protect both civil society *and* politics from the growing power of wealth.[43] Yet for these theorists, the power that wealth wields in the political sphere is understood only as the power to purchase. According to Rawls, the rich gain disproportionate sway over campaign outcomes and political decisions through their contributions. Walzer likewise criticized the tendency of political life to assume the form of a marketplace in which influence is for sale to whomever is willing and able to trade economic goods for political goods. As Cass Sunstein has put it, democracy depends on a basic distinction "between market processes of purchase and sale on the one hand and political processes of voting and reason-giving on the other."[44] The power of money, the theory goes, is a transactional power—a power, as Jean-Jacques Rousseau put it, to "make commerce of the public freedom."[45]

A mounting political-science literature on the role of money in American politics likewise traces the power of money to its capacity to purchase political power. Though direct quid pro quo exchanges may be rare, there are numerous less direct means by which the wealthy buy influence. A disproportionate electoral voice can be acquired through investment in opinion-shaping institutions.[46] The rich can and do incline representatives to vote their way by means of well-funded, well-organized lobbying efforts.[47] The wealthiest citizens have historically succeeded in beating back adverse policy initiatives through the aggressive use of lawyers and consultants.[48] Thus, students of American politics, like political theorists, have conceptualized the problem of wealth in politics in terms of money's capacity to purchase political power. As Samuel Huntington wrote in his classic work on the American political tradition, money "becomes evil not when it is used to buy goods but when it is used to buy power."[49]

There is much at stake in our understanding the psychological sources of oligarchic power. Indeed, consideration of this facet of the power of wealth reveals a neglected set of concerns. If wealth commands power not just as a currency but also as an idol, it would seem important for political theorists to ask how such power might be curbed or contained. Perhaps those interested in the corrosive effects of money in politics should not limit their focus to the regulation of lobbying and campaign finance but instead should widen their scope to consider how modern democracies succeed or fail to divert public admiration away from wealth.

The core of this study is an analysis of three texts. In addition to Adams's two most significant works of political thought, *Defence of the Constitutions of Government of the United States of America* and *Discourses on Davila*, his retirement-era correspondence with Jefferson also receives extended analysis. As we will see, the Adams-Jefferson letters contain some of Adams's most probing reflections on the power of wealth and birth, and his thinking on this theme is clarified through his lively engagement with Jefferson's distinctive views.

A number of Adams's lesser known works appear at the periphery of my analysis. I attempt to shed light on his mature works of political theory by examining their antecedents in earlier works, including his 1765 *Dissertation on the Canon and Feudal Law* and his 1776 *Thoughts on Government*. I draw from his correspondence, with a special focus on those exchanges that are richest in political-philosophical content. My treatment of Adams's conception of "natural" aristocracy in chapter 2 is supplemented by an analysis of a series of letters written to John Taylor of Caroline, who wrote a book-length critique of Adams's *Defence*. Similarly, my treatment of Adams's correspondence with Jefferson is supplemented by analysis of his well-known correspondence with Benjamin Rush, an exchange that occurred at nearly the same time and covered similar subject matter. Finally, I seek to enrich my study of Adams's thought by examining his sharp criticism of a range of works in his library, including Jean-Jacque Rousseau's *Discourse on the Origin and Basis of Inequality among Men*, Mary Wollstonecraft's *An Historical and Moral View of the Origin and Progress of the French Revolution*, and the Abbé de Mably's *De la législation*.

There are two quite different methods of intellectual history that I have employed in these pages. First, I have sought to situate Adams's ideas within the context of the history of political philosophy, and more specifically within the history of philosophically probing attempts to understand the nature of oligarchic power. My overarching goal, as signaled above, is to recover Adams's fear of oligarchy and, along the way, to uncover his unique understanding of the psychological sources of oligarchic power. In order to highlight the originality of his ideas, I consider Adams's differences with such figures as Samuel Huntington, Robert Dahl, Alexis de Tocqueville, Thomas Jefferson, Adam Smith, James Harrington, Niccolò Machiavelli, Polybius, and Aristotle.

It would be premature, however, to attempt such a reconstruction of Adams's thought without first acknowledging an important objection. As discussed above, it has been contended that Adams, far from being a critic of oligarchic power, was an apologist for it. His most significant political writings, after all, were efforts to advocate for an English-style "balanced constitution" that would limit democracy to one *part* of government situated alongside aristocratic and monarchical elements.

So before I reconstruct Adams's theory of oligarchy in light of a broader history of political philosophy, I set the stage by situating Adams's writings in the immediate intellectual and political context of his time. In chapter 1, I consider Adams's *Defence of the Constitutions* within a transatlantic debate about the desirability of English-style balanced government—a constitutional model that attempted to counterpose the monarchic, aristocratic, and democratic social elements together within the same government. The debate was most pronounced in Paris in the years preceding the French Revolution, when Anglomanes who sympathized with balanced government defended the model from the attacks of French reformers. I argue that Adams, though a defender of a certain idea of balanced government, departed from the prevalent theory. Whereas conventional Anglomanes had emphasized the danger to such balance posed by the popular, democratic element, Adams was preoccupied instead with the threat to that balance posed by an overweening aristocratic class.

Having demonstrated Adams's preoccupation with aristocracy, I then proceed in chapter 2 to reconstruct his understanding of aristocratic power. By revisiting his debates with Thomas Jefferson and John Taylor of Caroline, I recover the reasoning behind Adams's bleak prediction that wealth and birth—and not talent and virtue—would enjoy the preponderance of power in republican America. I turn, in chapter 3, to the question of how, precisely, Adams understood wealth to translate into political influence. As previewed above, I draw from *Discourses on Davila* and other writings an understanding of oligarchic power that traces the political power of wealth not to the capacity of the rich to buy influence but instead to public admiration and sympathy for the rich.

The notion that oligarchic power derives in part from public admiration suggests that those seeking to mitigate oligarchy ought to consider the means by which modern democracies might divert admiration away from wealth. In chapter 4 I draw from Adams's writings to argue that the most effective means of diverting admiration from wealth might be to create and maintain offices and stations that, by virtue of the honor they bestow, enjoy the admiration of the public. Meritocratic judgeships and high elected offices, when honor is attached to them, might compete with the grandeur of wealth for public admiration. As we will see, the spirit of Adams's political thought warns against the democratic impulse to knock down honorable institutions. A democratic political community might believe it is equalizing conditions by electing judges and secretaries of high office rather than appointing them, or by regulating political offices with highly restrictive limits on the duration and number of terms, but the unintended consequence of attempts to bring offices closer to the people might be the elimination of the only markers of social distinction that can compete with wealth for the admiration of the public. Adams captured the point succinctly in his notes on Mary Wollstonecraft's *An Historical and Moral View of the Origin and Progress of the French Revolution*. Responding to Wollstonecraft's attack on the distinctions of prerevolutionary France, Adams warned that "the distinction of property will have more influence than all the rest in commercial countries, if it is not rivalled by some other distinction."[50] Adams's political thought serves as a warning that the egalitarian impulse to empty offices of their honor might have the unanticipated effect of increasing the already immense influence of wealth in modern democracies.

CHAPTER ONE

A Perennial Problem

It is that rapacious spirit described by the elder
Adams; and no one understood the true character of a
purse-proud, grasping oligarchy better than he did.

—SENATOR JOHN MILTON NILES,
speech delivered in the US Senate, 18 February 1838[1]

SHOULD AMERICANS FEAR OLIGARCHY? In other words,
should citizens of a republic founded upon ideals of civic
equality fear the political power of the rich? Even if this question is being asked today with a special urgency, the question itself is hardly new. At the outset of the American republic, when
the framers of the United States Constitution first submitted
the document to the public for approval, the question of oligarchy was hotly debated. Critics of the Constitution—the so-
called Anti-Federalists—argued that the new system would
elevate to power a wealthy ruling class. Rather than empowering those "who have been used to walk in the plain and frugal
paths of life," the new system of government would guarantee
rule by America's "aristocracy." What the Constitution's defenders had fancifully called "representative democracy" would
in fact be "a mere burlesque." There would be "no part of the people represented, but the rich," and no security provided against
the undue influence of a social and economic elite.[2]

Meanwhile, Federalist proponents of the Constitution argued that there was little reason to view the rich as a dangerous

political force. After all, the aristocratic orders of the Old World were absent in post-Revolution America, and the Constitution mandated that this remain the case by expressly prohibiting titles of nobility. America would be a *republic*, and the real danger in republics was not oligarchic power but the power of untrammeled majorities. James Madison, whose influence at the Philadelphia Convention was second to none, warned against "the superior force of an interested and over-bearing majority." In his monumental tenth essay in the *Federalist Papers*, Madison paid only passing attention to the danger that an oligarchic elite could pose. Being small in numbers, such an elite would simply be voted down. Oligarchic power might exist as a nuisance, but it would not be a serious threat to the republic: "It may clog the administration, it may convulse the society; but it will be unable to execute and mask its violence under the forms of the Constitution."[3] In a revolutionary republic that had thrown off aristocracy and monarchy and put "We the People" on the throne, there was no reason to fear oligarchy.

When Federalists and Anti-Federalists debated the likelihood of oligarchy in America, they were partaking in a larger, transatlantic discourse about how best to ameliorate the vast inequality of political power that had characterized the aristocratic societies of eighteenth-century Europe. The emerging democratic-republican consensus, espoused by an increasingly influential set of reformers in France and several other European nations, held that the key to eliminating aristocratic privilege was the dismantling of the various forms of *legal* privilege found in European societies. Orders of nobility, titles, social ranks or "estates," hereditary magistracies—these were the pillars that propped up aristocratic privilege. Pulling down such pillars would be the essential step in breaking aristocratic power and establishing true republics, formed upon the basis of equal citizenship.[4]

From the perspective of the American Federalists, the Constitution of 1787 would establish just the type of republic envisioned by European reformers. The proposed American system prohibited titles of nobility and—remarkably in the context of the eighteenth century—made no distinction between the rich and the poor. In this context, what did Anti-Federalists mean when they spoke of a home-grown aristocracy? They agreed that America would be home to an aristocracy in the ancient-Greek sense of *hoi aristoi* (the best), a class of men distinguished by meritocratic qualities such as talent and virtue. But with the entrenched aristocratic orders of the Old World completely absent in America, the fear of a dangerous aristocracy or oligarchy of corrupt elites was without foundation.

Yet leading Federalists and European reformers alike tended to overlook a dissenting view of elite power. In the American context, many Anti-Federalists believed that the roots of political inequality ran deeper than was assumed and that aristocratic power would survive the dismantling of formal aristocratic institutions. When Anti-Federalists used the term "aristocracy," they meant something quite different from the conventional aristocracy of the Old World. Though formal aristocratic orders would not exist in the new republic, America would remain threatened by an oligarchic elite consisting of "birth, education, talents, and wealth," a class that would tend to monopolize political power. This class, which Anti-Federalists insisted on calling an aristocracy, would lack the trappings of European nobility but would nonetheless enjoy distinctions "as visible and of as much influence as titles, stars and garters."[5]

The problem of aristocracy was among the chief points of contention during the ratification debates of 1788, as Federalists and Anti-Federalists argued the merits of the proposed Constitution. The tension reached a peak at the New York State Ratifying Convention, when Alexander Hamilton vigorously assaulted the notion that an aristocracy existed in America. The fiercely ambitious, self-made Hamilton, who by the age of thirty-three had bootstrapped himself from obscure origins to wealth and notoriety, dismissed his opponents' fears of aristocracy as mere paranoia. It was true that some men were distinguished by qualities such as wealth and wisdom and that others were not, but such distinctions alone did not set men apart from one another politically. Not only did the Constitution proscribe titles of nobility, it also drew no political distinction between social or economic classes. In this context it was delusional to describe the American elite as an ominous ruling class. "This description, I presume to say, is ridiculous. The image is a phantom. Does the new government render a rich man more eligible than a poor one? No."[6]

Roughly eighteen months before Hamilton dismissed his opponents' fears of oligarchy, John Adams had begun work on his three-volume *Defence of the Constitutions of Government of the United States of America*. The *Defence* was motivated by a variety of events and provocations, but among Adams's chief goals from the very outset was that of articulating the threat that aristocracy had posed to political communities throughout history. In the midst of a democratic-republican revolution that was transforming the Atlantic world, Adams sought to impress upon reformers and revolutionaries his conviction that the power of social and economic elites would not vanish with the abolition of formal titles of nobility.

Adams was still in Europe when Hamilton stood up at the New York Ratifying Convention to deny the presence of an oligarchic threat. We can only imagine how the distinguished New Englander might have responded. We know that he was, by that time, a firm supporter of the proposed Constitution;[7] however, he probably would have objected to the view of Hamilton and others that the Constitution would be invulnerable to domination by elites. In fact, the likelihood of Adams's dissent from the mainstream Federalist position was suggested by the immediate Anti-Federalist rejoinder to Hamilton's argument. The rejoinder fell to upstate lawyer and merchant Melancton Smith, the leading Anti-Federalist present at the convention. Plainspoken, disheveled in appearance, and from an undistinguished family, Smith was no match for Hamilton in flair or oratory, but he persisted in warning the delegates of an oligarchic American elite. Perhaps in recognition of the mismatch in stature between Hamilton and himself, Smith defended the Anti-Federalist description of aristocracy by invoking a distinguished authority: "My idea of aristocracy is not new:—It is embraced by many writers on government:—I would refer the gentleman for a definition of it to the honorable *John Adams*, one of our natural aristocrats."[8]

Indeed, close examination of Anti-Federalist writings suggests that several of the most influential Anti-Federalists drew their critique of aristocracy from Adams's *Defence*. Adams shared not just Melancton Smith's belief in the existence of an oligarchic elite, but also his fear that such an elite would dominate American political life. As we will see, the *Defence* was in large part an effort to describe the threat posed by aristocratic power, a threat that had persisted through the ages and would remain even in an age of republican equality. Aristocrats would continue to wield enough power to subvert the institutions of government, even in the context of popular sovereignty and unicameral assemblies. Eliminating the vestiges of monarchical and aristocratic orders would not solve the perennial problem of aristocratic power.

POLITICAL HERETIC

John Adams's most careful readers would eventually discover that he was a sharp critic of what the ancient Greeks called

oligarchy, meaning rule (*arche*) by the few (*oligos*). C. Wright
Mills found in Adams a shrewd critic of the power and status
of elites.[9] Likewise, the political theorist Judith Shklar identified Adams as the source of a longstanding American tradition
of decrying and criticizing elite domination.[10]

And yet this characterization would likely have surprised
many of Adams's contemporaries. By the time the debate over
the proposed Constitution was raging, Adams's *Defence* had left
many with the impression that he was committed to the aristocratic and monarchical institutions of the old world. After all,
the first volume could be read as a defense of institutions resembling the British Crown and the House of Lords. Far from
a critic of oligarchy, Adams appeared to be an apologist for aristocratic forms, calling for the embodiment in government of
the aristocratic and monarchic elements of society. When James
Madison first read Adams's *Defence* in the summer of 1787, he
feared that that the work would "revive the predilections of this
country for the British Constitution," and he wished that "the
remarks in it which are unfriendly to republicanism may not
receive fresh weight from the operations of our governments."[11]
Madison's cousin, the Reverend James Madison, went further. In
publishing the *Defence*, Adams was "insidiously attempting . . .
to overturn our present Constitutions . . . plotting Revolutions."
The reverend surmised that Adams, having spent so much time
abroad, had been infected by the charms of monarchy. "I fear
his Optics have been too weak to withstand the Glare of European Courts."[12]

This perception was not wholly ungrounded. Adams's *Defence*
was a vigorous argument in favor of the ancient idea of balanced
government, which the British constitution was widely thought
to embody. Adams originally set out to write the work in response to a published letter penned by the celebrated French finance minister Anne-Robert-Jacques Turgot. Writing in 1778,

Turgot had assaulted several of the American constitutions for their seeming imitation of the British model of balanced government. With independent governors and bicameral legislatures, the configuration of power in several of the American states closely resembled the British balance between the king, the Lords, and the Commons. Instead of forming a true republic, "formed upon the equality of all citizens" and requiring that all authority be brought "into one, that of the nation," the Americans had imitated the English balance, "as if the same equilibrium of powers which has been thought necessary to balance the enormous preponderance of royalty, could be of any use in republics."[13] Adams, from the very beginning, intended his treatise as a defense of the equilibrium of powers that Turgot so detested. His *Defence* was an apology of sorts, aimed at those, especially in America, who "entertained sentiments similar to these of M. Turgot."[14]

By responding to Turgot, Adams was entering a great transatlantic debate over the merits of balanced government. Should the corrupt monarchical and aristocratic structures of Europe be replaced by something like the balanced constitution of Britain, or should reformers reject the idea of balanced government altogether in favor of a republican model of unified national sovereignty? In debating the merits of balanced government, eighteenth-century writers confronted an ancient idea elaborated most succinctly by the Greek historian Polybius.[15] According to him, the three basic constitutional forms were each intrinsically unstable. Given time, monarchy (rule by the one), aristocracy (rule by the few), and democracy (rule by the many) would each decay, respectively, into corrupt rule by the one (tyranny), the few (oligarchy), or the many (mob rule). The key to avoiding corrupt government was to replace "simple and uniform" constitutions with a balanced form that brought together "all the good and distinctive features of the best governments." Such a scheme ensured that "none of the principles should grow unduly and be perverted into its allied evil." Balanced government prevented decay by way of a balance of power that neutralized "the force of each" against that of the others.[16]

In the Atlantic world of the eighteenth century, the British constitution stood as a living example of the ancient theory. Beginning in the seventeenth century, it had become common for Englishmen to understand the institutions of the king, the House of Lords, and the House of Commons in terms of the classical theory of balanced government.[17] The British system gained an international reputation in the mid-eighteenth century with the publication of Montesquieu's *The Spirit of the Laws*.[18] For Montesquieu, as for many English interpreters, the British constitution had avoided domination by the democratic element of society by instituting a "body of the nobles" as a separate part of the legislative power. "In a state," he wrote, "there are always some people who are distinguished by birth, wealth, or honors." If mixed with the common people in a single chamber of government, men of this class would lose interest in the state. Most acts of legislation would oppose them, and therefore "the common liberty would be their enslavement and they would have no interest in defending it." The only way to keep the nobles attached to government was to follow the British example and erect a House of Lords, a body that would grant them political advantages proportionate to their social advantages.[19]

Whereas radical French reformers like Turgot and Condorcet rejected this line of reasoning, Montesquieu's praise of the British constitution became a bedrock for the conservative Anglomanes. To give one prominent example, Montesquieu's theory was presented to the Constituent Assembly of 1789 by the Anglomane politician Gérard de Lally-Tollendal. In the first concrete plan submitted to the assembly, Lally-Tollendal proposed a second legislative chamber whose members would be appointed for life by the king. Defending his proposal in the terms of Montesquieu's doctrine, Lally-Tollendal argued that by dividing legislative power among competing social elements, the constitution would strike a perfect equilibrium, thereby avoiding domination by any single class interest.[20]

John Adams's readers would understandably interpret his *Defence* as aligned with the Anglomane thought of the period. From the first pages of the work, Adams drew quite heavily on Jean Louis De Lolme's *The Constitution of England*.[21] And indeed, Adams's *Defence* would itself become something of a touchstone for European Anglomanes. When Gérard de Lally-Tollendal proposed an English-style system of balanced government to the French Constituent Assembly in 1789, he appealed to Adams's *Defence* for support.[22]

Adams's association with Anglomane ideas was especially damning considering that by the late 1780s the intellectual current of the Atlantic world had turned decisively against notions of balanced government. It was an ideological turn centuries in the making. Advocates of absolute sovereignty, such as Jean Bodin and Thomas Hobbes, had argued powerfully against the division of governmental power among social classes. Stable and authoritative rule required that legislative authority emanate from a single, undivided source.[23] And by the late eighteenth century, the absolutist line of argument took a democratic turn as arguments for a united, *popular* sovereignty gained widespread appeal. Across Europe and even in the American colonies prior to the Revolution, the role of nobility in society and politics faced heightened scrutiny as noble status became increasingly associated with monetary wealth and as nobles were increasingly viewed as using their privileged access to government to multiply personal fortunes.[24] To divide up the people's sovereignty and to grant a part of it to a self-dealing nobility was an insult to republicanism. As Jean-Jacques Rousseau put

it, defenders of balanced government were like those Japanese
conjurers who "cut a child to pieces before the eyes of the audience; then, throwing all the members one by one into the air,
they cause the child to fall back again, alive and perfectly reas-
sembled." Rousseau intimated that even if a child could survive
such a stunt, a republican political community would not be so
lucky.[25]

   In the context of this current of democratic-republican thinking, Adams's sympathy for institutions balancing the one, the
few, and the many could be interpreted as reactionary. This was
no less true in America, where the proposed Federal Constitution broke decisively with the theory of balanced government.
To be sure, the Constitution resembled models of balanced government in its checks and balances, bicameralism, and separation of powers, but the idea of competing social classes partic-
ipating alongside one another in legislation—an idea central to
balanced-government thought—was left behind by Federalist theory. The new Constitution did not situate social classes
alongside one another in a state of equilibrium. Instead, as Federalists argued, the new system was one of *popular sovereignty and
representation*. Where balanced governments divided legislative
authority between one, few, and many, the proposed Constitution united all authority and lodged it in a single sovereign people. Even as governmental power was parceled out to multiple
branches and legislative chambers, officials of all agencies ultimately derived their power from the electorate.[26]

   It was true that the presidency appeared to be endowed with
the power and majesty of a monarch, and that the Senate, with
fewer members, longer terms, and an indirect relation to the
people, appeared to be intentionally elevated above the lower
house in prestige and importance. But contrary to appearances,
the Constitution's framers insisted that their new system abandoned all classical notions of divided sovereignty.[27] Unlike the

House of Lords, which granted a part of legislative power to a social elite, the US Senate was popular in its derivation, with no property qualification and with its members chosen by popularly elected state legislatures.[28] Similarly, the presidency lacked both the hereditary claims and the "sacred and inviolable" quality of the British king. To the contrary, as Alexander Hamilton was keen to point out, the chief magistrate was "amendable to personal punishment and disgrace" through periodic elections.[29] Moreover, executive power was placed in a single person not to institutionalize society's monarchical element, but rather to generate the *energy* required for effective use of executive power. Decision, activity, secrecy, and dispatch—all qualities "conducive to energy"—tended to be found in one man to a greater extent than in groups.[30] Like the Senate, the presidency lacked any tie to classical notions of divided sovereignty. The new system clearly parceled out power to multiple branches and legislative chambers, but all powers ultimately derived from the people. Unlike the model of balanced government that Adams advocated for in his *Defence*, the Constitution gave no institutional role to "the one" or "the few."

Subtle though it may seem, the distinction between British-style balanced government and American checks and balances was not lost on Adams's first American readers. Shortly after the first appearance of the *Defence* in America, there appeared a scathing critique of the work, entitled *Observations on Government*, which was written under the pseudonym Farmer of New-Jersey and believed at the time to be the work of New Jersey governor William Livingston. The author was in fact John Stevens, a wealthy New Jersey farmer who would eventually win renown as an inventor. Stevens attacked Adams's *Defence* for presenting the American republics as miniatures of the English system of balanced government. In spite of their various separations and divisions of power, Stevens argued, the American republics were essentially democratic. The division among the "several component powers of government" did not reflect class divisions but were merely guards against the consolidation of power by any one man or body of men.[31]

Stevens's critique eventually made its way across the Atlantic and into the hands of the Marquis de Condorcet and his fellow reformer Pierre Dupont, who saw in the critique an opportunity to draw on the cachet of American republicanism in order to discredit Adams's writings and, by extension, the British model of government.[32] Condorcet and Dupont promptly translated and published the pamphlet under the title *Examen du gouvernement de l'Angleterre*, adding to it extensive commentary of their own. In the summer of 1789, when the Constituent Assembly debated whether to institute a British-style bicameral legislature and an absolute royal veto, Stevens's critique—which was still believed to be the work of William Livingston—was repeatedly cited by opponents of the British model and pitted against the work of "the Anglo-American" John Adams. The Duke de la Rochefoucauld announced that just as "Montesquieu could be refuted by Rousseau," Adams could be refuted by "Livingston."[33] While Stevens's pamphlet came to represent the cause of popular sovereignty, Adams's *Defence* was associated with the reactionary demand for a politically privileged elite capable of constraining the popular will. Adams, called by one delegate "a blind partisan of the inequality of rights,"[34] was labeled an antiquated thinker defending obsolete notions of balanced government.

Adams may not have predicted the scale of the confusion, but he did anticipate that readers would misunderstand him. Upon completion of the first volume of the *Defence*, he lamented to his close friend and fellow revolutionary James Warren: "Popularity was never my mistress, nor was I ever, or shall I ever be a popular man."[35] Adams's wife Abigail, who had read the manuscript and discussed its principles at length, warned that readers would perceive the author to be agitating for mon-archy.[36] Writing to Benjamin Franklin, Adams struck a tone of defiance. The *Defence*, he wrote, "contains my confession of political faith, and, if it is heresy, I shall, I suppose, be cast out of communion."[37]

Adams's closest readers could discern a grave error in the popular perception of his writings. At the heart of the matter was a failure to see that Adams was no conventional Anglomane. To be sure, the casual reader of the *Defence* discovers without difficulty numerous passages defending something quite like an aristocratic senate and a unitary executive resembling the British monarch. However, a closer look at the *Defence* and its influences reveals that Adams departed significantly from traditional defenders of the balanced constitution. Central to Adams's peculiar defense of balanced government was a preoccupation with the threat posed to republican government by oligarchic elites.

OSTRACISM

As we have seen, by the time Adams published the *Defence*, it was commonplace to view the institutions of balanced government as obsolete and even, for many, as antirepublican. After all, according to conventional versions of the theory, the social elements comprising "the one" and "the few" were to be granted privileged roles in government. For Adams to defend such a system appeared to many as a rearguard effort to hold back the tide of democratic-republican reform and to preserve the aristocratic privilege of the Old World.

Yet anyone who closely examined Adams's view of balanced government would find that his peculiar version of the theory defied common perceptions. Indeed, the most seemingly aristocratic elements of his theory of balanced government—the

dignified Senate and the strong chief executive—were in fact
designed to prevent aristocrats from undermining republican
institutions. Whereas the conventional theory of balanced government had conceived of the Senate in conventional terms as
an independent mediator of the conflict between monarch and
people, Adams presented the chamber not as a mediating body
but rather as an *ostracizing* body. "The rich, the well-born and the
able," he wrote in the preface to the *Defence*, inevitably "acquire
an influence among the people that will soon be too much for
simple honesty and plain sense, in a house of representatives."
Adams's solution was to corral the most distinguished citizens
into a single chamber—one *part* of government, thereby pre-
venting them from dominating *all* of government.[38]

It is not that Adams's constitutional theory was *anti*aristocratic. Indeed, Adams believed that the same type of individual
who threatened to dominate the people could be of greatest use
to them when controlled by institutions. By isolating the aristocrat in an upper chamber, the people could "hope for the benefits of his exertions, without dreading his passions." But even
if the Senate could be a "reservoir of wisdom," appointment to
the Senate was, in an important sense, a demotion rather than
an honor. It was "to all honest and useful intents, *an ostracism*."
Through senatorial appointment, the aristocrat was relegated to
a position in which he "can govern very few votes more than his
own among the senators." As an example of how such an appointment would control aristocracy, Adams described the way
in which the influence of both William Pulteney and William
Pitt was diminished by appointment to the House of Lords.[39]

Just as the theme of aristocratic domination can be read in
Adams's discussion of the Senate, the same theme was pronounced in his defense of a strong unitary executive. Adams's
well-documented sympathy for a dignified executive has been

taken as proof of an outmoded and even antirepublican conception of politics.[40] Yet a close look at Adams's writings on executive power suggests that his executive, like his Senate, was intended less as a station of privilege than as a bulwark against
aristocratic domination. While he conceived of the Senate as a
body serving to ostracize ambitious individuals, he came to understand the executive office similarly as the protector of the people against those same men of ambition. Among the chief lessons that Adams drew from his survey of political history was
that the popular, representative character of government relied
upon a powerful chief magistrate. Wherever executive power
was not placed in a dignified and unitary office, popular government would fall under the mastery of the most distinguished
citizens.

Adams's theory of executive and senatorial power was probably influenced by the political writings of De Lolme, whose
Constitution of England Adams called "the best defence of the
political balance of the three powers that ever was written."[41]
Just as Adams has often been misread as an apologist for aristocracy, De Lolme has been interpreted by historians as a prop-
agator of the conventional eighteenth-century theory of balanced government. His *Constitution*, first published in English
in 1775, appeared to many merely as a more comprehensive version of Montesquieu's famous commentary on the English constitution in *The Spirit of the Laws*. It is true that De Lolme's theory, like Montesquieu's, combined a separation of powers with
a balance of the social orders of king, nobility, and people.[42]
Yet in a manner that John Adams would adopt, De Lolme
altered the nature of the balance. According to the classical
English model, the perennial political struggle was between
king and people, with the Lords sitting in between as a mediating body. De Lolme, who suffered the rule of oligarchs in

his native Geneva,[43] departed from Montesquieu by singling out aristocracy, rather than the people or the monarch, as the primary source of disorder in republics. For De Lolme, the perennial political struggle was not between people and king, but between people and aristocracy. The king, according to De Lolme's theory, was not the people's antagonist but rather their protector. Tasked with sheltering the common citizenry from the overweening ambition of the aristocrats, the king replaced the aristocracy as the constitutional balancer.[44]

In his *Constitution*, De Lolme presented appointment to the House of Lords as a means of controlling aristocrats. By granting a preeminent member of the House of Commons a seat in the House of Lords, De Lolme wrote, the English constitution, "in the very reward it prepares for him, makes him find a kind of Ostracism."[45] The putative advance of "the favourite of the people" to that distinguished body "is at the same time a great step towards the loss of that power which might render him formidable." Once a lord, he loses much, if not all, of his influence with the people. Upon seeing that he no longer derives his greatness from their favor, the people grow jealous of his privileged position and begin to "lessen their attachment to him."[46] As merely one of many lords, he can no longer enjoy the special prestige associated with the word *first*. Moreover, as the favorite of the people, the extent of his greatness is indeterminate and therefore boundless. As a lord, by contrast, his greatness is placed within bounds through the grant of fixed privileges, and thus "his value is lowered, just because it is ascertained." Yet despite all of these disadvantages, the aristocrat will still be induced by the offer of dignity to take a seat in the upper house. Aristocratic characters will willingly trade their status as favorites of the people for the dignities of lordship.[47] De Lolme summed up the constitution's treatment of the man of ambition with an analogy to a reservoir's taming of a violent torrent:

> His advances were sudden, and his course rapid; he was if you please, like a torrent ready to bear down every thing before it, but this torrent is compelled, by the general arrangement of things, finally to throw itself into a vast reservoir, where it mingles, and loses its force and direction.[48]

For De Lolme, as it would be for Adams, a dignified upper house ostracizes the aristocracy by inducing the most distinguished citizens to trade power for pageantry.

De Lolme thought the British monarch performed a similar function. In the *Constitution*, the notion of a dignified executive as a bulwark against aristocratic tyranny is elaborated at length. After citing Machiavelli's *History of Florence* to the effect that the history of republican government is one of domination by oligarchies of ruling families, De Lolme argued that the English constitution had avoided that fate through the institution of royal authority. Beyond the familiar function of executing the law, De Lolme thus gave the chief executive a counter-aristocratic function.[49] Denying the potential attribution of monarchism to his writings, De Lolme insisted that "the power of the Crown in England stands upon foundations entirely different from those on which the same Power rests in other Countries."[50] Royal authority served to prevent the rise of oligarchs by concentrating the people's reverence on one individual. By investing the head of state "with all the personal privileges, all the pomp, all the majesty, of which human dignities are capable," the constitution renders it impossible for any citizen "to rise to any dangerous greatness."[51] The institution of one "very great man," De Lolme writes, places a strong check on those who would strive for greatness, and thereby prevents those disorders which "in all Republics, ever brought on the ruin of liberty, and before it was lost, obstructed the enjoyment of it."[52]

Adams followed De Lolme in understanding the chief magistrate to be the natural ally of the people. For evidence of this alliance, Adams cited the writings of King Stanislaus of Poland, who at length lamented the "state of extreme humiliation" to which his nation's people had been driven under the oppression of the nobles. The people paid the taxes, labored in the fields, gathered the crops, manned the armies, and generally supported the necessities, pleasures, and luxuries of the nobility. And yet, as the king recounted with horror, the populace had "fallen from all the rights of humanity," a reality highlighted by the law that imposed a mere fine of fifteen livres on a gentleman for killing a peasant. King Stanislaus stopped just short of calling for open rebellion, noting that if "a masculine and daring spirit" were to rise among the people, no barrier would be strong enough to oppose them. After all, as the king noted, it was "open force" that enabled the plebeians of Rome to establish the tribunes, which "balanced the power of the nobility." Prior to this assertion of power, the plebeians had been in a state of servitude, subject to the violence of the patricians.[53]

Adams intimated that if the king's authority had been less circumscribed in Poland, a healthy alliance might have materialized between the king and the people. It was a political maxim for Adams that democratic power existed in a mutually supportive relationship with unitary executive authority. Instead of James I's famous statement "no bishop, no king," wrote Adams, it was more truthful to say "no people, no king, and no king, no people."[54] For the people to retain a place of authority in the constitution, they needed a chief magistrate to defend them against the grasping aristocracy.[55] "What is the whole history of the wars of the barons," Adams asked, "but one demonstration of this truth?"[56] In republican government, the executive "is the natural friend of the people, and the only defense which they or their representatives can have against the avarice and ambition of the rich and distinguished citizens."[57]

If Adams's readers viewed him as an apologist for aristocracy, this was only because they ignored his view of how the institutions of balanced government were supposed to operate. In his view, they functioned above all to control society's social and economic elite, a class that Adams would later describe as "the most difficult animals to manage of any thing in the whole theory and practice of government."[58]

And yet, insofar as Adams's contemporaries did understand his peculiar rationale for balanced government, they were not convinced by his institutional prescriptions. This is understandable, given that Adams never provided a compelling argument as to how it would be possible to ostracize elites in their own governmental chamber without simultaneously granting them excessive political power. How could citizens be so sure that elites, once appointed to the Senate, would be substantially disempowered? Writing many years later, Thomas Jefferson reasonably warned that Adams's design for controlling the oligarchs would likely have unintended consequences:

> I think that to give them power in order to prevent them from doing mischief, is arming them for it, and increasing instead of remedying the evil. For if the coordinate branches can arrest their action, so may they that of the coordinates.[59]

From the outset, Adams's ostracism scheme was vexed by the probability that an aristocratic senate would be more likely to empower elites than to control them.

But if Adams's critics could dismiss ostracism as an institutional scheme, they could not so easily dismiss the deeper problem that ostracism was meant to solve.[60] For Adams, all republics throughout history had been vulnerable to aristocratic domination. Aristocracy was therefore a perennial problem of political life, a problem that would not vanish in a new age of democracy. As we will see, Adams's institutional design was only a derivation of the central point he wished to convey: that even in the wake of the republican-democratic revolution—even once the aristocratic forms of the old world were abolished—the problem of aristocratic power would stubbornly persist.

The Annals of Oligarchy

Adams's use of the term "aristocracy" designated a class of men who, in the classical terminology, would be more accurately described as oligarchs. In the classical republican tradition of thought, an elite ruling class could be either benign or corrupt. If virtuous, noble, wellborn, or all of the above, members of the ruling class were designated part of an aristocracy. If corrupt, self-serving, and grasping for power, the ruling few were instead called an oligarchy. By using a single term interchangeably, Adams eschewed the classical distinction between a morally salutary aristocracy and morally blameworthy oligarchy. In this respect, he followed the Florentine writer and diplomat Niccolò Machiavelli, who understood the elite few simply as "the great," and who departed from the mainstream tradition of republican thought with his insistence that it was elites and not tyrannical majorities who posed the principal threat to the health of republics. Machiavelli characterized the common people, or *popolo*, as relatively honest and decent in their motives, as they desired not to dominate or oppress others but "only *not* to be commanded or oppressed." The elite, by contrast, harbored less wholesome motives. Much like the class of men whom Adams would call "the most difficult animals to manage," Machiavelli's *grandi* were driven by a desire "to command and oppress the people." It was with this understanding of class politics in mind that Machiavelli praised institutions and practices that would control elites and render them accountable to the people.[61]

In these respects, Adams adhered to Machiavelli's ideas to an extent that was rare among his contemporaries. For most Founding Era students of politics, it was Montesquieu who had done the most to synthesize ancient and modern political philosophies and it was Montesquieu's *Spirit of the Laws* that could be drawn upon as a font of political wisdom. But Adams wrote that "*Machiavel* was the first who revived the ancient politics" and that Montesquieu was largely derivative of Machiavelli, having "borrowed the best part of his book from *Machiavel*, without acknowledging the quotation."[62] It appears that Adams took special pains to absorb the lessons of Machiavelli and other Italian historians. While composing the second volume of the *Defence*, which exclusively dealt with the histories of the Italian republics, Adams taught himself Italian, spent a small fortune acquiring scarce histories from London bookstores, and worked such long hours at his desk that Abigail feared for his well-being.[63] Writing to Jefferson, he noted that "it has cost me a great deal of expense to search into Italian rubbish and ruins"; however, he wrote, "enough pure gold and marble has been found to reward the pains."[64]

Adams's adherence to Machiavelli's class politics was not without qualification. He rejected the Florentine's sharp distinction between the root desires of the few and those of the common people. In the *Defence* he castigated Marchamont Nedham for his flattery of the many: "It is very easy to flatter the democratical portion of society by making such distinctions between them and the monarchical and aristocratical; but flattery is as base an artifice and as pernicious a vice, when offered to the people, as when given to the others." Just as there was no reason to follow the apologists for aristocracy by attributing benevolence to the few, it was likewise a mistake to attribute any special honesty to the people. After all, "they are all of the same clay; their minds and bodies are alike."[65] Additionally, as we will see in chapter 4, Adams departed from Machiavelli by holding out promise that the energies of "the few" could in fact be harnessed for the good of the republic. And yet, we will see that in spite of these important differences, Adams followed Machiavelli quite closely in his emphasis on the special danger posed by socioeconomic elites.

Adams drew most extensively from Machiavelli's *History of Florence*, a text that elaborated in detail the tendency of republics to devolve into elite tyranny.[66] In a passage cited by Adams, Machiavelli told of a popular uprising defeating one of Florence's noble families. Having succeeded in suppressing the "pride and insupportable ambition" of the nobles, Florence's citizens believed civic harmony would ensue. Instead, the factious spirit of nobility did not die but was transferred to a new faction of citizens that quickly endeavored "to render themselves masters of the republic." Machiavelli relates the lesson learned by his Florentine narrator: "It seems almost necessarily ordained, in order that in human affairs there may be nothing either settled or permanent, that in all republics there are what may be called fatal families, born for the ruin of their country." As soon as one factious class of nobles was suppressed, another inevitably sprang up to take its place.[67] Adams drew from Machiavelli the lesson that distinguished individuals and families will threaten the constitutional order regardless of whether any formal nobility is recognized. From Florence's "series of alternate tragedy, comedy, and farce," Adams wrote in the *Defence*, we learn that although "nobles were all excluded from the government, the exclusion was but a form." Try to "exclude the aristocratical part of the community," he said, and "they will still govern the state underhand." Formal democracy results in de facto oligarchy. Elected officials will be mere tools of the most distinguished citizens, and "in constant fear of them, will behave like mere puppets danced upon their wires."[68]

On the surface, Adams's *Defence* was an effort to defend bicameralism and a strong chief executive against the criticism of Turgot. But deeper down, Adams had set out to impress on his readers the persistent reality of aristocracy and the threat it posed to republican government. For Adams, the proof of the stubbornness of elite power lay in the rich history of republics from ancient Sparta to his native Massachusetts. Indeed, Adams's *Defence* was in large part an effort to collect and catalog the annals of oligarchy. Much of the work, especially the first two volumes, consists of a historical recounting of episodes in which members of a powerful elite worked to undermine effective republican government.[69]

There were two main avenues by which aristocrats had historically undermined republics. First, they subverted popular representation by concentrating in their own hands the power of legislative assemblies. And second, they inhibited the effectiveness of government by stripping away the authority of chief executives, thereby transforming once-effective governing offices into ceremonial posts.

There was no clearer way to corrupt a republic than to hollow out the *representative* character of its popular assembly. Adams viewed popular representation as the hallmark of republican government. As he would later write in a letter to his cousin Samuel Adams, the term *republican* designated "a government in which the people have collectively, or by representation, an essential share in the sovereignty."[70] He agreed with James Harrington that the interest of the people was synonymous with the *public* interest, and that "where the public interest governs, it is a government of laws, and not of men." For the public interest to govern, Adams believed it was necessary for the representative assembly to be a "mirror" of the public, sharing a likeness of sentiments and interests with the people. As he had written in his *Thoughts on Government* (1776), the representative assembly "should be in miniature an exact portrait of the people at large. It should think, feel, reason and act like them."[71]

Genuine representation, wherever it had been established, was an exceedingly fragile achievement. The threat of aristocratic subversion was never far off. Adams warned that in all republics with any degree of commercial development, "an aristocracy has risen up in a course of time, consisting of a few rich and honorable families, who have united with each other against both the people and the first magistrate." And furthermore, the aristocrats had inspired the people "with so mean an esteem of themselves, and so deep a veneration and strong attachment to their rulers, as to believe and confess them a superior order of beings."[72]

Indeed, so difficult was the establishment of representation in the face of aristocratic power that it was only very recently, in the popular assemblies of the American states, that a complete representation of the people had been achieved. Adams viewed the establishment of popular assemblies in post-Revolution America as a world-historical achievement, the culmination of an arduous history of efforts to wrest power from ruling aristocracies. The origins of the modern popular assembly could be traced to the founding of Sparta, when the lawgiver Lycurgus sought to counterbalance the power of hereditary oligarchy by instituting popular assemblies. Yet, as Adams pointed out, Lycurgus fell short of true representation by excluding the assemblies from debate and limiting their role to that of confirming or rejecting the proposals of the senate. Citizens in the assemblies "were to give their simple ayes or noes, without being allowed to speak, even so far as to give a reason for their vote."[73] Similarly, the Roman republic sought to secure the plebeians in their ongoing contests with the patrician class by instituting the tribunes, officers "vested with such privileges and authority as enabled them to become arbiters betwixt those two estates" and capable of curbing the insolence of the patricians.[74] Yet much like Sparta's assemblies, the Roman tribunes proved inadequate as protectors of the people's interests. "An assembly of representatives," wrote Adams, "would have had an equal right with the senate to propose laws, to deliberate, debate, alter, amend, improve." The tribunes, by contrast, "were authorized only to forbid any measure they thought injurious; but not to propose any law, or move any resolution." Without adequate power to protect the people, the tribunes were strong enough only "to head every popular tumult, and blow up every spark to a flame."[75]

More recently, under the reign of King Charles VII of France and in other feudal monarchies, commoners had sought protection from aristocracies by forming standing armies around kings. The people, "harassed to death by the domination of noble families . . . surrounded the throne with troops" in an effort to humble their superiors. This strategy, however, offered limited security. Without acquiring power "in their own hands," the people were "still subject to as much aristocratical domination as the crowns think proper to permit."[76]

It was not until the advent of modern representation in England that popular power was reliably secured from aristocratic domination. In spite of its extraordinary wealth and imperial power, England had refused a standing army and, by the strength of its institutions, had "preserved the power of the people." England had reduced to practice an idea foundational to the theory of republican government: that "the property of the people should be represented in the legislature, and decide the rule of justice." The system of representation that had emerged in England gave hope that rule by aristocratic junto was not the inevitable fate of republics.[77]

For all of the ridicule Adams endured for his admiration of the British constitution, often overlooked were the actual reasons underlying his admiration. Chief among these was the system's successful establishment of popular power. He did not think that representation in Britain was flawless. Indeed, he believed that even as Britain had made great strides in establishing popular representation, the British parliament remained plagued by the corrupt borough system, which disregarded population size in granting seats and which enabled the rich to buy seats for relatives and personal favorites who often resided outside of the borough. Nonetheless, Adams held out hope that the British system of representation might be purified. By redrawing districts in proportion to population and by allowing only inhabitants of a given district to be chosen for office, reform might make the commons "an immortal guardian of the national liberty."[78]

It was in the American states that true popular representation was fully realized. The American constitutions, Adams wrote, would "prove themselves improvements, both upon the Roman, the Spartan, and the English commonwealths."[79] The thirteen governments, each with a popular assembly free of the corruption found in the British constitution, were "the first example of governments erected on the simple principles of nature," because they were "founded on the natural authority of the people alone."[80]

America's popular assemblies had granted the people more true authority than they had possessed even in democratic Athens. Commenting on the experience of that ancient democracy, Adams noted that the democratic power it exhibited was "amiable, noble, and I had almost said, divine." Yet the people of such a democracy, not holding power as part of a well-ordered constitutional system, were "but a transient glare of glory, which passes away like a flash of lightning." Without the aid of a balanced government enabling them to preserve their share of power, the people were "like a momentary appearance of a goddess to an ancient hero, which, by revealing but a glimpse of celestial beauties, only excited regret that he had ever seen them."[81] In contrast, the stability and constancy of popular power in the American assemblies meant that the people of America had "more real authority than they had in Athens." The assemblies were truly democratic in that intrigue for office was relatively uncommon and election was not confined to rank or wealth. And at the same time, being spread over a large territory and unable to meet in one assembly, the people were "not exposed to those tumultuous commotions, like the raging waves of the sea, which always agitated the ecclesia at Athens." It was an open question "whether a government so popular can preserve itself." But the gamble was well worth it. If the American experiment proved successful, there would be reason to hope "for all the equality, all the liberty, and every other good fruit of an Athenian democracy, without any of its ingratitude, levity, convulsions, or factions."[82]

In his commitment to durable popular representation, Adams resembled those reformers and revolutionaries, from Turgot to the Abbé Sieyès, who clamored for genuinely representative government. However, Adams departed from the revolutionary demand that bicameral legislative assemblies be replaced with unicameral assemblies. Turgot had argued that the inclusion of nobility in an upper legislative chamber would corrupt the representative character of government. Adams argued, to the contrary, that unicameral assemblies were *more* vulnerable to aristocratic subversion than bicameral ones. "The progressive march of all assemblies," he insisted, was toward a consolidation of power in the hands of an oligarchy, as men of "a few noble families" pursued their own ambitious designs and eventually excluded the people from government entirely. One prominent example of this tendency was the republic of Geneva, the history of which, Adams wrote, "deserves to be studied with anxious attention by every American citizen." In Geneva, the "fatal slumbers of the people" and their "invincible attachment to a few families" opened the door to domineering aristocratic passions, as men of aristocratic families were moved by "cool deliberate rage . . . to grasp all authority into their own hands."[83]

Turgot and his circle had intimated that it was the formal powers of nobility—the institutional embodiment of aristocracy—that undermined genuine representation. But the case of Geneva suggested that the aristocratic threat would persist even under democratic conditions. After all, Geneva's aristocrats had risen to power through democratic elections. Once warm in their seats, the aristocrats became "loth to leave them, or hold them any longer at the will of the people." Only then did they maneuver to pass a law that would allow the two councils of the assembly to elect one another, thereby creating two ruling councils that were "perpetual, and independent of the people entirely." In this way the representation of the people disappeared from Geneva, as the aristocratic order of magistrates "soon learned to consider their authority as a family property, as all others in general, in similar circumstances, ever did, and ever will." Important for Adams, the capacity of Geneva's aristocrats to transform a republic into an entrenched oligarchy was not owing to their formal privileges, but instead was "characteristic of this order of men in every age and nation."[84]

The threat to popular representation would not vanish with the abolition of hereditary magistrates, for even if all political offices were made elective, aristocrats would dominate elections. Among any electorate, wrote Adams, some will be "profligate and unprincipled," willing to "sell or give away their votes for other considerations than wisdom and virtue." This fact greatly advantaged those ambitious few "who should think themselves most distinguished by blood and education, as well as fortune"— those men who, when facing opposition to their election, could easily resort to "entertainments, secret intrigues, and every popular art, and even to bribes" in order to carry the election. For Adams, it was "a natural and unchangeable inconvenience in all popular elections . . . that he who has the deepest purse, or the fewest scruples about using it, will generally prevail."[85]

If the radical reformers had ignored the historical tendency of aristocrats to undermine popular representation, they had also ignored the tendency of aristocrats to obstruct government by undermining the authority of chief executives. Just as the elite few could be counted on to outfox the people, they tended also to exceed the first magistrate in their cunning and to make of him "a mere ceremony." Adams repeatedly referred to the doge of Venice as a model case of the tendency of the executive to be turned by aristocrats into a ceremonial office, lacking altogether in real political authority. Moved by the ambition to prevent the prince from allying with the people against the nobility, and likewise to prevent the people from "applying to the doge for assistance," the sagacious nobles of Venice managed to flatter the prince into trading authority for dignity. The nobles, who "always know at least the vices and weaknesses of the human heart better than princes or people," enticed the prince to give up his status as an independent executive by offering him "the frivolous distinction of living in the ducal palace." Once a first magistrate, Venice's head of state became only the first among equals.[86]

The history of Poland from the fifteenth through the seventeenth centuries provided a premier example of the tendency of the aristocracy to encroach upon the crown and to strip away "one prerogative after another, until it was reduced down to a mere doge of Venice." The greatest of all blows suffered by royal authority in Poland was the liberum veto. Introduced under the reign of John Cassimer, the measure granted each representative the power "to interpose a negative" and thereby to break up the lawmaking assembly. The veto was supported by a coalition of groups, all of which shared an interest in fomenting confusion and inaction in the assembly: state officials seeking to avoid enquiries into their administration, nobles seeking to prevent the imposition of new taxes or to avoid conviction for capital crimes, and foreign powers seeking to take advantage of confusions in the Polish councils.[87]

Though some had called the liberum veto "the dearest palladium of Polish liberty," the measure eventually reduced Poland to a state of lawlessness and destitution. With the king having lost all authority and the nobles "in a state of uncontrouled anarchy," Poland became home to "the greatest inequality of fortune in the world; the extremes of riches and poverty, of luxury and misery, in the neighbourhood of each other . . . a country without manufactures, without commerce, and in every view the most distressed in the world."[88]

For all its misfortune and extreme inequality, Poland was just one example of a universal tendency of nobles "to scramble for diminutions of the regal authority, to grasp the whole executive power, and augment their own privileges." In Poland, as in Venice and many other polities, the nobles had "attained a direct aristocracy, under a monarchical name, where a few are above the controul of the laws, while the many are deprived of their protection."[89]

This threat—that aristocrats could work diligently to diminish executive authority—was one that Adams would actively seek to mitigate. During his tenure as vice president and sitting president of the Senate, Adams became convinced that without the power of removal, presidential authority would be dangerously curtailed by the aristocratic Senate.[90] A similar fear would motivate him years later, during his retirement, when Senator James Hillhouse of Connecticut publically proposed a sweeping set of amendments to the Constitution. Hillhouse, a wealthy Federalist and arch-opponent of the Jeffersonians, proposed to diminish turbulent "party spirit" by reducing the duration of terms in both houses of Congress, by abolishing the vice presidency, and, above all, by reconstituting the presidency, weakening its prerogatives of appointment and renewal and mandating that the president be selected from among the Senate.[91] In a review of the Hillhouse proposal, Adams exclaimed that he could not imagine "a project more perfectly aristocratical." The executive, an office already too intermingled with the Senatorial powers, would be further stripped of its independence, to the point of resembling a doge of Venice—the model of executive impotence that Adams had cited repeatedly in his *Defence*.

Hillhouse had seemed to believe that the Senate and executive needed to be more closely conjoined if democratic tyranny was to be avoided. In an effort to illustrate the much greater threat posed by *aristocratic* tyranny, Adams called to mind biblical imagery of beasts of prey and fiery furnaces. "Unless protected by the strong arm of monarchy," Hillhouse had written, "as well might a man take up his abode in a tiger's den." To this Adams snapped back: "I say, as well might a man take up his abode with Shadrach, Meshech, and Abednego, in the fiery furnace, as democracy with aristocracy, without the strong arm of monarchy to protect it." And he went further: "as well might a man take up his abode with Daniel in the lion's den as monarchy with aristocracy, without the million arms of democracy to defend it." It was not that aristocracy posed the only danger: "All these jealousies exist in some degree," wrote Adams. But as we have seen, he believed that the greatest jealousy of all was that harbored by aristocrats toward executive power. "Aristocracy is the natural enemy of monarchy," he wrote, "and monarchy and democracy are the natural allies against it."[92]

It was in light of the long history of aristocratic domination that Adams defended the institutions of balanced government. Only a bicameral legislature and a powerful independent executive could mitigate the threats posed to both popular representation and the rule of law. In the *Defence* Adams considered how his native Massachusetts might be governed under a constitution like the one called for by Turgot, a constitution in which the features of balanced government were absent and all authority was concentrated in a unicameral assembly. As in Geneva, the most distinguished citizens could be counted on to seek election to the assembly, and "nineteen in twenty of them" would win. Once in office, those men of distinction "most inflamed with ambition and avarice . . . most vain of their descent" could be counted on constantly to "endeavor to increase their own influence, by exaggerating all the attributes they possess, and by augmenting them in every way they can think of." Moreover, those representatives resembling the common class of citizens would become "humble imitators" of the most distinguished. "Notwithstanding all the equality that can ever be hoped for among men," the people's representatives would generally defer to the aristocratic man, whether because they would be "afraid of his influence in the districts they represent, or related to him by blood, or connected with him in trade, or dependent upon him for favors." And in addition to undermining popular representation, the aristocracy would also undermine the authority of the highest office. Among the aristocracy, wrote Adams, there would be several whose "fortunes, families, and merits" approach the highest level. Out of "the ordinary delusions of self-love and self-interest," such aristocrats would be "much disposed to claim the first place as their own right." Eventually, Adams predicted, those wishing for the head office but unable to obtain it would "endeavor to keep down the speaker as near upon a level with themselves as possible, by paring away the dignity and importance of his office, as we saw was the case in Venice, Poland, and, indeed, everywhere else."[93]

Adams concluded the first volume of his *Defence* by addressing Turgot's political theory directly. Turgot's system of government, though purportedly grounded on human equality, would in fact carry with it "all the inequalities and disputes that he so greatly apprehends." His assembly would inevitably fall under the influence of "a few grandees" who would reliably combine with one another to carry elections, set procedures, and exempt themselves from taxes and arrests. "In a word," wrote Adams, "as long as half a score of capital characters agree, they will gradually form the house and the nation into a system of subordination and dependence to themselves, and govern all at their discretion—a simple aristocracy or oligarchy in effect, though a simple democracy in name." Meanwhile, if the "capital characters" of Turgot's assembly should come to disagree with one another, they would "keep the nation anxious and irritated, with controversies which can never be decided nor ended." They would quarrel among themselves and also with the first magistrate, and would "excite clamors and uneasiness, if not commotions and seditions" against the head of state, thereby weakening the authority of the office that is "the natural friend of the people, and the only defence which they or their representatives can have against the avarice and ambition of the rich and distinguished citizens."[94] In short, single-assembly government would result in both oligarchy and anarchy—in the domination of the political process by the distinguished few and also the undermining of the basic functions of government. Such was the lesson to be culled from the annals of oligarchy.

When Adams's friend and fellow diplomat Thomas Jefferson first shared his view that the newly proposed Constitution bore an eerie resemblance to monarchy, Adams insisted to the contrary that the new system more closely resembled an aristocracy and that he would have "given more power to the President and less to the Senate." His constitutional difference with Jefferson could therefore be summed up as a disagreement about whom to fear: "You are afraid of the one, I, the few."[95]

It was an article of faith among democratic-republican reformers, from Turgot to Jefferson, that oligarchic power was a vestige of obsolete systems of rule. Strip away the old orders and distinctions, form republics upon the principle of equality, and the age-old threat posed by social and economic elites would recede into history. From Adams's perspective, the reformers failed to perceive the deep roots of political inequality. They had conflated aristocratic power with aristocratic forms, when in reality the problem of power was deeper and more stubborn than the problem of forms. To Adams's ongoing frustration, the conflation would persist into the early republic. Thus, even when Jefferson and the Jeffersonians decried the power of "the few," they tended to view elite power in America as linked to a resurgence of an "anglo-monarchical" political order.

As we will see, reformers and revolutionaries tended to overlook the deeper problem of aristocratic power in part because they thought that in the absence of corrupt aristocracies of the Old World, there would spring up a benign, meritocratic elite—an elite consisting of the wise, virtuous, and talented. In other words, the detested aristocracy of titles would be supplanted by a praiseworthy aristocracy of merit. As we will see in the following chapters, Adams went to great lengths to disabuse his contemporaries of this notion. Throughout history, it was not qualities of merit that had been the primary bases of aristocratic power, but instead qualities of *fortune*, such as birth, beauty, and wealth. And the power of fortune—especially the power of wealth—had deep roots not just in material-economic relations but also in the human psyche. What all of this amounted to was a dire warning that the danger of political domination by social and economic elites would not vanish in an age of formal equality. Efforts to build a more egalitarian republic would require an honest reckoning with the nature of oligarchic power.

CHAPTER TWO

The Goods of Fortune

Now, my friend, who are the *aristoi*? Philosophers may
answer, "the wise and good." But the world, mankind,
have, by their practice, always answered, "the rich, the
beautiful, and well-born." And philosophers themselves,
in marrying their children, prefer the rich, the handsome,
and the well-descended, to the wise and good.

—JOHN ADAMS TO THOMAS JEFFERSON,
2 September 1813

ADAMS'S PREOCCUPATION WITH ARISTOCRATS alienated
him from all but a few of his contemporaries. Few would
insist as Adams did that social and economic elites would continue to endanger republican institutions long after the prohibition of aristocratic titles. Even Adams himself, writing about
his native Massachusetts, admitted that aristocratic forms were
a thing of the past. Gone were the "artificial inequalities of condition, such as hereditary dignities, titles, magistracies, or legal
distinctions."[1] And yet, as we have seen, Adams went on warning of a powerful aristocracy that if left unchecked would undermine the functions of republican government.

But what did this stubborn statesman-scholar mean by "aristocracy"? What kind of aristocracy was it that could survive in
spite of republican equality? For those Founding Era Americans
versed in the classical republican tradition, there was a simple
answer: in the absence of those *artificial* aristocracies erected by

THE GOODS OF FORTUNE 59

corrupt governments, there could still exist a "natural" aristocracy. In other words, there could be a class whose elite status did not derive from a legal framework but instead from natural talents, abilities, and qualities of character. Among the most remarkable statements on the idea of natural aristocracy were those from Adams's foremost ideological antagonist, Thomas Jefferson. As we will see, Jefferson envisioned a republic of merit, in which the vestiges of Old World aristocracy would be swept away and in which an educated citizenry would freely elect to be ruled by the most talented and virtuous.

Adams too spoke of a "natural aristocracy" that would supplant the artificial aristocracies of old, but he redefined this term. He argued that the natural aristocrat was simply the person to whom power flowed naturally even in the absence of formal privileges. It was a mistake, he insisted, to assume that without aristocratic titles and ranks, power would flow to the best and the brightest. Power would instead accrue, as if by a perverse law of nature, to the wealthy and wellborn. These were the true natural aristocrats, and with Adams's redefinition of natural aristocracy came a reevaluation of its role in the republic.

"You and I Ought Not to Die"

In 1812, years after both men had retired from public life, John Adams and Thomas Jefferson began a conversation that has been hailed as "one of the great correspondences in the history of American letters."[2] For a dialogue between two politicians, the correspondence is remarkable and even perhaps unmatched in its philosophic depth. The exchange spanned a wide range of subject matter, delving into deep reflections on education, religion, history, language, diplomacy, politics, and numerous other fields. The letters strike a remarkably contemplative tone, removed from the rough and tumble of practical politics. Setting the tempo early on, Jefferson notified Adams that he had "taken final leave" of active political life. "I have given up newspapers in exchange for Tacitus and Thucydides, for Newton and Euclid; and I find myself much the happier."[3]

A correspondence between the ex-presidents was an unlikely event. While they had been close political allies as early as the Continental Congress and had cultivated a deep friendship while serving as fellow diplomats in Europe in the 1780s, the bond between them was severed by the partisan convulsions of the 1790s that culminated in the election of 1800. That election, one of the bitterest and most vitriolic in American history, had pitted Adams and Jefferson against one another as the respective standard-bearers of two starkly opposed ideologies. Both men could claim irreparable damage. Jefferson had been maligned as an atheist and an enemy of the Christian faith and as a coward who, while serving as governor of Virginia during the revolution, had fled enemy forces and abandoned his compatriots. Meanwhile, Adams had suffered the vile character attacks of Jefferson's hired propagandists, who had gone so far as to call Adams—the sitting president—a "hideous hermaphroditical character which has neither the force and firmness of a man, nor the gentleness and sensibility of a woman."[4] The decade following Jefferson's momentous victory had been one of cold silence between the two. The closest they had come to contact during the period was a short, cool exchange of letters between Jefferson and Abigail Adams, in which Abigail informed Jefferson that she no longer esteemed his character and reprimanded him for stooping so low as to fund the vicious attacks of the propagandist James Callender, a "serpent" who had since turned his venomous pen on Jefferson himself.[5]

When the two finally reconciled after the persistent prodding of a mutual friend, there was one sharp disagreement that still remained.[6] At issue was Adams's commitment to the cause

of republican self-government. There was no question about
his early role as a champion of the revolutionary cause. But
had the erstwhile revolutionary undergone a change of heart
while abroad in Europe, serving as minister to the Court of
St. James? Jefferson had long thought so. As he would write in
his political memoirs, Adams "had originally been a republican" but had been moved by the disorder of Shays' Rebellion
and the "glare of royalty and nobility" to defend unrepublican
institutions in writing and, upon his return to America, to ally
with "the monarchical federalists."[7]

At the start of a long series of recollections over their respective roles in the convulsions that accompanied the early republic, Jefferson noted that the two men stood on opposite sides of
an eternal contest. Since "the first origin of societies . . . in all
governments where they have been permitted freely to think
and to speak," wrote Jefferson, the same question had convulsed
society: "whether the power of the people, or that of the *aristoi*
should prevail." The political terms "whig and tory," wrote Jefferson, "belong to natural, as well as to civil history. . . . They
denote the temper and constitution of mind of different individuals." Jefferson recollected that he and Adams had been together
on the side of the people during the contests of the Continental Congress, and both had in 1787 supported a Constitution
with amendments.[8] But once the new government was up and
running, the two men found themselves "separated for the first
time" as the respective leaders of two parties, "each wishing to
give a different direction to the government"—one aligned with
the many, the other the few. Reaching out to Adams, Jefferson
suggested that their earlier differences were partly due to circumstances: "Every one takes his side in favor of the many, or
of the few, according to his constitution, and the circumstances
in which he is placed." But in Jefferson's mind there still was no
mistaking the divergence between Adams and himself. Jefferson

had allied with the party aiming "to strengthen the most popular branch," whereas Adams had led efforts to empower "the
more permanent branches, and to extend their permanence."[9]

Jefferson's version of the story, in which he cast himself as
the champion of democracy and Adams as the apologist for
aristocracy, gained widespread acceptance during his own lifetime and after. Considering the contrasting origins and life-
styles of the two men, these were odd characterizations. Jefferson, not Adams, was the slave-owning aristocrat living a life of
opulence entirely cloistered from the experience of the average
citizen. Adams, by contrast, had sprung from middling origins,
had never acquired great wealth, and had lived plainly even
after acquiring fame. Nonetheless, Jefferson's early leadership
of the Republican opposition had secured his status as a man of
the people. Meanwhile, Adams's political writings and actions
had provoked his critics—and especially his political opponents—to paint him as a monarchist and a defender of hereditary aristocracy.

From the outset of the correspondence, Adams was eager to
correct the record. "You and I ought not to die," he told Jefferson, "before We have explained ourselves to each other."[10] As
we will see, in an important sense it was Adams, not Jefferson,
who was the consistent critic of aristocratic power. For unlike
Jefferson, who predicted that Old World aristocracies would be
replaced in the republican age by new natural aristocracies of
virtue and talent, Adams believed that wealth and family name
would continue to overpower virtue and talent, and therefore
that the danger of aristocratic domination would remain even
in a well-ordered republic.

As we have seen in chapter 1, John Adams did *not* believe that
the democratic-republican revolution would defeat aristocratic
power. Just as they always had, the wealthy and wellborn would
continue to constitute a powerful elite class, even in the absence

of formal privileges. In taking this position, Adams predicted a different future than his hopeful contemporaries. The Jeffersonians envisioned the preponderance of power shifting away from a privileged, undeserving aristocracy. In a well-ordered republic, virtue and talent would replace wealth and birth as the qualifications for high office. It was in response to Jefferson's vision of a meritocratic republic that Adams would develop and elaborate his own predictions about elite power in America.

JEFFERSON'S MERITOCRATIC REPUBLIC

Following a sporadic string of short letters from Adams on the topic of aristocracy, Jefferson finally responded in the form of an elegant, comprehensive essay, as if intending to put the issue to rest. "I agree with you that there is a natural aristocracy among men." Jefferson insisted that there were two types of aristocrat: one natural, characterized by virtue and talents, and the other artificial, "founded on wealth and birth." It was true that artificial aristocracy was "a mischievous ingredient in government" and that "provision should be made to prevent it's [*sic*] ascendancy," but the same could not be said of the natural aristocracy, whom Jefferson considered "the most precious gift of nature for the instruction, the trusts, and government of society." To the contrary, the mark of a well-ordered polity was its capacity to filter natural aristocrats into leadership roles. "May we not even say that that form of government is best that provides most effectually for the pure selection of these natural aristoi into the offices of government?" Jefferson thought that everything from a polity's land laws to its educational system should be structured to achieve this basic filtering function.[11]

Jefferson's idea of the role and character of aristocracy was consistent with a broader strain of late-eighteenth-century republicanism. Thomas Paine had drawn a sharp contrast between the talent and knowledge of the rising elite, on the one hand, and the "visible imbecility and want of intellects" of the old aristocracy, on the other. The old aristocracy was "rather jeered at as an ass, than dreaded as a lion"—despised more, in other words, for its lack of merit than for its natural strength. "This," Paine wrote, "is the general character of aristocracy, or what are called Nobles or Nobility, or rather No-ability, in all countries."[12]

According to Paine, republican reformers now believed that elite status should rest on a new basis, that "rank and dignity in society must take a new ground. The old one has fallen through.—It must now take the substantial ground of character, instead of the chimerical ground of titles."[13] The ideal of substituting merit for artificial privilege became especially pronounced among those "liberal" republicans who, several years into the French Revolution, wished to end the upheaval and to establish a stable republic. The influential liberal novelist, socialite, and political theorist Madame de Staël believed that the key ingredient in a stable French republic would be the Conserving Body, a meritocratically selected chamber of government consisting of distinguished statesmen, intellectuals, and military officers. Staël did not deny that the Conserving Body would be essentially aristocratic. "Yes, it is an aristocratic institution," she wrote, but aristocratic only in the sense of "government of the best." It would be composed of "the natural aristocracy, in opposition to the artificial aristocracy." Indeed, the natural aristocrats would be "the destroyers and the irreconcilable enemies" of artificial aristocracy.[14]

In the early years of the American republic, many saw no contradiction between popular sovereignty on the one hand and leadership by a meritocratic elite on the other. James Wilson, a framer of the Constitution who loudly and persistently defended the idea of popular sovereignty, believed aristocracy—insofar as it was understood in meritocratic terms—was a salutary element of representative government. Wilson insisted that the Anti-Federalists, who had raised the specter of an ominous aristocratic class, were operating on false definitions. In a speech at the Pennsylvania Ratifying Convention, Wilson examined the meaning of "aristocracy" by turning to the etymology of the word: "When we trace it to the language from which it is derived, an aristocracy means nothing more or less than a government of the best men in the community." Representation by a natural aristocracy differed from what Wilson called aristocratic government, a system of rule in which a select body of men held power either electively, hereditarily, by territorial possessions, "or some other qualifications that are not the result of personal properties." By "personal properties" Wilson did not mean wealth but rather "the qualities of the head and the disposition of the heart." The natural aristocracy, insofar as it existed, did not consist of a formally privileged class but instead of "those most noted for wisdom and virtue." So defined, Wilson found no objection to the employment of the natural aristocracy in representative government.[15]

Indeed, many of the foremost theorists of the emerging system of representative democracy expected the electorate to play the central role in enabling meritocratic rule. Jefferson envisioned an enlightened electorate that would distinguish between the authentic and the pseudo aristocrats, making sure that those who reach office are "the real good and wise."[16] The ideal of a vigilant electorate standing ready to guard meritocratic institutions from oligarchic incursions had been articulated forcefully in the *Federalist* essays of James Madison, who would later become Jefferson's chief confidante as well as one of the chief formulators and propagators of the Jeffersonian political vision. Madison wrote in *Federalist* 57 that the first aim of every political constitution is "to obtain for rulers men who possess most wisdom to discern, and most virtue to pursue, the common good," and he believed that in the new republic the electorate would achieve this aim. In *Federalist* 10, Madison praised large electoral districts for their tendency not only to break up powerful factions but also to *enlarge*, rather than simply mirror, the views of constituents "by passing them through the medium of a chosen body of citizens."[17] In his earlier career, when preparing to draft a plan for a new constitution that would serve as a starting point for the deliberations of the 1787 convention, Madison sought a mode of selecting representatives that would "extract from the mass of the Society the purest and noblest characters which it contains."[18] With this goal in mind, Madison's original model for the Senate called for senators to be selected not by the people or their state legislatures but instead by the national House of Representatives, which would choose from nominees submitted by the state legislatures. Such a complex scheme of selection was meant to elevate an elite that could stand above factional conflict, serving as what Madison elsewhere called a "disinterested & dispassionate umpire in disputes between different passions & interests."[19]

When Anti-Federalists argued that under the new system the House of Representatives and the Senate alike would be filled by a narrow class of elites whose interests would run counter to those of the people, Madison retorted that the people could be counted on to guard against an "elevation of the few on the depression of the many." For one thing, the people would hold elected officials accountable through what political scientists would later call retrospective voting. In the event of a betrayal of the public trust, the electorate would be prepared to review an official's exercise of power and to determine whether "a faithful discharge of their trust shall have established their title to a renewal of it." Moreover, a vigilant electorate would prevent corrupt officials from winning office in the first place by carefully selecting for office those whose merit made them eligible for "the esteem and confidence" of the country. As Jefferson would later put it, a vigilant electorate would stand prepared to perform the "separation of the aristoi from the pseudo-aristoi, of the wheat from the chaff."[20]

It was not that these visionaries perceived no threat from oligarchic elites. To the contrary; in the early years of the republic Jefferson became the figurehead and chief instigator of an opposition movement decrying the emergence of an elite, antirepublican faction. With Madison as his chief lieutenant, Jefferson led an ideological charge that consciously recalled the "anti-court" opposition movement of early-eighteenth-century England. Just as Viscount Bolingbroke had decried the corruption of England by an alliance between government and an emerging financial oligarchy, the Jeffersonians mobilized against the emerging Hamiltonian financial system. Just as anti-court ideologues had denounced the corrupt dealings of Robert Walpole—his dependency on the emerging systems of banking and credit and his efforts to consolidate power by corrupting the legislature—the Jeffersonians denounced Hamilton's efforts to establish centralized banking, public credit, and state-sponsored industrialization. And just as the anti-court movement had identified a parasitic class of moneyed men and stockjobbers who had latched onto Walpole, the Jeffersonians pointed to an oligarchic group of conspirators circling around Hamilton. "A sect has shewn itself among us," Jefferson wrote to Lafayette in the summer of 1792, "who declare they espoused our new constitution, not as a good & sufficient thing itself, but only as a step to an English constitution, the only thing good & sufficient in itself, in their eye."[21] The sect would achieve its monarchist designs through a corrupt Walpolean alliance between centralized government and financial elites—or, in the Jeffersonian parlance, an alliance between king-jobbers and stockjobbers.[22]

Bolingbroke had feared that Walpole's financial revolution would undermine the power and eminence of England's landed gentry. For Jefferson, the fear was for the fate of republican self-government. What the politics of the early republic amounted to, Jefferson wrote, was a contest of principle "between the advocates of republican, and those of kingly government." Madison, articulating the Jeffersonian critique in the *National Gazette* in 1792, distinguished between a republican government that derived its energy "from the will of society" and a corrupt government that operated by "converting its pecuniary dispensations into bounties to favorites, or bribes to opponents;" by "accommodating its measures to the avidity of a part of the nation instead of the benefit of the whole"; and, finally, by

> enlisting an army of interested partizans, whose tongues, whose pens, whose intrigues, and whose active combinations, by supplying the terror of the sword, may support a real domination of the few, under an apparent liberty of the many.[23]

Though the Republican Party had overwhelming strength in numbers, enjoying the allegiance of "the mass of people in every part of the union, in every state, and of every occupation," its political fortune was not secure. "Whether the republican or the rival party will ultimately establish its ascendance," wrote Madison, "is a problem which may be contemplated now; but which time alone can solve." If one party could claim the support of the numerical majority, the other could count among its camp an alternate source of influence in an active and zealous economic elite:

> The antirepublican party . . . being the weaker in point of numbers, will be induced by the most obvious motives to strengthen themselves with the men of influence,

particularly of moneyed, which is the most active and insinuating influence.

The men of moneyed influence could make up in intrigue what they lacked in numbers by constantly scheming to divide their opponents in order to prevent the formation of general coalitions. Even in a republican system, numbers would not automatically defeat powerful minority factions. As Madison noted, "Experience shews that in politics as in war, stratagem is often an overmatch for numbers."[24]

Yet, while Jeffersonians believed that oligarchy posed a threat to the early republic, they remained confident that this threat could be quelled by institutional reform and that the republic could be ordered in such a way as to elevate the natural aristocracy of talent over its oligarchic counterpart. Jefferson believed that his own native Virginia had already succeeded in undercutting the oligarchic power of the landed elite by reforming the laws of entail and primogeniture. Writing to Adams, he touted as his own handiwork Virginia's land reforms, laws that "laid the axe to the root of Pseudo-aristocracy."[25] But the most important reform of all in this regard would be that of the education system. An enlightened system of education promised to undercut oligarchy and to shift power to the people and their meritocratic representatives. Jefferson had long believed that education could facilitate the selection of virtue and talent by teaching the electorate to weed out tyrannical ambition. In the preamble to his 1778 "A Bill for the More General Diffusion of Knowledge," a bill he had proposed in the Virginia House of Delegates, he had predicted that education would

> illuminate, as far as practicable, the minds of the people at large, and . . . give them knowledge of those facts, which history exhibiteth, that possessed thereby of the experience

of other ages and countries, they may be enabled to know ambition under all its shapes, and prompt to exert their natural powers to defeat its purposes.[26]

"Common" schools would educate future voters at the public expense and "without regard to wealth, birth, or other accidental condition or circumstance." As recounted in his *Notes on the State of Virginia*, Jefferson proposed to divide every county into wards of five or six square miles and to establish a school in each ward, free for three years of study. Students would learn the necessary skills of reading, writing, and arithmetic. Importantly, their reading would be "chiefly historical," because a study of "the experience of other times and other nations . . . will qualify them as judges of the actions and designs of men."[27] As Jefferson wrote to Adams, he believed this common education would both prepare citizens for the activity of local government and also fulfill "the great object of qualifying them to select the veritable aristoi, for the trusts of government, to the exclusion of the Pseudalists."[28]

Jefferson's system of education would also supply a natural aristoi that could stand for election. His original education bill had provided for those students deemed "of the best and most promising genius and disposition" to be elevated to the highest levels of education "at the common expense of all" and "without regard to wealth, birth, or other accidental condition or circumstance."[29] The vision of an elite class drawn from all ranks of society and cultivated for leadership was one that recalled a long tradition of republican thought. The seventeenth-century English political writer James Harrington insisted in his utopian treatise *Commonwealth of Oceana* that the true natural aristocracy was not one of social rank but was instead "diffused by God throughout the whole body of mankind," a claim that made imperative the careful training and selection of leadership.[30] Indeed, the ideal harkened all the way back to Plato's *Republic*. As Socrates tells it, in an ideal republic, citizens should be made to believe that men, like metals, vary in caliber. Some are born of gold or silver and therefore fit for honor and command, whereas others are born of brass and iron and are better suited for farming and craftsmanship. Though such a social-political hierarchy was divinely ordained, and though men of gold caliber were meant to rule, it was not to be assumed that gold fathers would beget gold sons, nor that brass or iron fathers would *not* beget gold sons. It was therefore of utmost importance that members of the elite "guardian" class carefully discern the caliber of newborn offspring, so that when it came time to select future guardians they would not neglect the occasional golden child born of brass pedigree.[31]

What writers in the classical republican tradition had only dreamed of, Jefferson actively sought to make a reality. According to his vision, twenty poor children of superior talent would be "raked from the rubbish" each year, the best of whom would eventually attend the elite College of William and Mary at public expense. By such means, Jefferson assured Adams, "Worth and genius would thus have been sought out from every condition of life, and completely prepared by education for defeating the competition of wealth and birth for public trusts."[32]

FORTUNE AND POWER

Adams yearned for an opportunity to engage Jefferson on the topic of aristocracy. At the outset of their renewed correspondence, Adams recalled a conversation between him and Jefferson from decades before, when both were serving as diplomats in Paris. "I recollect, near thirty years ago," Adams wrote to Jefferson, to have said carelessly to you, that I wished I could find time and means to write something upon aristocracy. You seized upon the idea, and encouraged me to do it with all that friendly warmth that is natural and habitual to you. I soon began, and have been writing upon that subject ever since. I have been so unfortunate as never to be able to make myself understood.[33]

Adams's first extended effort to clarify his understanding of aristocracy had appeared in the *Defence*. As we have seen in chapter 1, the *Defence* described in detail the threat posed by aristocracy by cataloging the many historical episodes when aristocrats undermined republican institutions. Beyond the description of the threat posed by aristocrats, Adams also sought in the *Defence* to describe the nature of aristocratic power. In a remarkable passage nestled within a critical discussion of the ideas of Franklin and Turgot, Adams reflected on the sources of elite power—what it was, in other words, that had enabled aristocrats to threaten republics throughout history. Adams recognized that in every political community "there are great inequalities of merit, or talents, virtues, services, and what is of more moment, very often reputation." The most meritorious, he insisted, had always enjoyed considerable weight in public opinion and in public deliberations. This, he wrote, "will be readily admitted."[34] Less obvious, but no less true, was the fact that in all known political communities, a great deal of power flowed to certain individuals on account of the very qualities that Jefferson had attributed to the "pseudo-aristocrats": wealth and family background. Just as in the hierarchical societies of the past, birth and wealth continued to be sources of power even in egalitarian New England.

Adams wrote at length on the persisting influence of birth. "Let the page in history be quoted, where any nation, ancient or modern, civilized or savage, is mentioned, among whom no difference was made between the citizens, on account of their extraction." Those of distinguished birth enjoyed influence through the veneration that naturally accompanied illustrious family names and through the considerable early advantages they enjoyed in education. From early childhood, the wellborn were acquainted with public characters and exposed to public affairs. The power of birth was a fact that all men simultaneously derided and respected. "Go into every village in New England," he wrote, "and you will find that the office of justice of the peace, and even the place of representative, which has ever depended only on the freest election of the people, have generally descended from generation to generation, in three or four families at most."[35]

Citizens of Massachusetts continued to hold certain family names in high esteem even as they grew suspicious of their rulers. Adams recounted a conversation he witnessed in which a man was "haranguing on the jealousy which a free people ought to entertain of their liberties." But as soon as the discussion turned to a critique of the governor of Massachusetts, the same jealous republican suddenly became deferential. "The present governor," Adams recorded the man as saying, "has done us such services, that he ought to rule us, he and his posterity after him, for ever and ever." Adams noted that even though the man's opinions seemed logically inconsistent, the reality was that his deference to family lineage was rooted in something deeper than logic. "His jealousy was the dictate of his understanding. His confidence and enthusiasm the impulse of his heart."[36]

The power of birth was a theme that Adams would return to again and again in his political writings, and it was a pronounced theme in his letters to Jefferson. Months before Jefferson would respond with his own idea of aristocracy, Adams prodded him by citing ancient texts in order to demonstrate that men had been attracted to family lineage since the sixth century BC. Translating Theognis from the original Greek, Adams found the ancient poet to believe that men were as likely to value the family lineage of human beings as they were to value good breed in farm animals. "Nobility in men is worth as much as it is in horses, asses, or rams."[37] Plato's *Republic* provided further testament to the longstanding advantages of the wellborn. According to Adams, it was in response to inequalities of birth that Plato had infamously recommended that wives be shared in common, that family lineage be erased, and that relations between sons, fathers, and brothers be extinguished. Despite the absurdity of Plato's prescriptions, Adams thought it important to appreciate that "no Man ever expressed so much terror of the Power of Birth."[38]

Even more potent than birth as a source of aristocratic influence was wealth.[39] A rich man without family prestige, Adams suggested, was more influential than a wellborn man without riches.[40] A key mechanism for the translation of wealth into political influence was the relationship of material dependency between the poor and the rich. "It will be easily conceived," Adams wrote, "that all the rich men will have many of the poor, in the various trades, manufactures, and other occupations in life, dependent upon them for their daily bread; many of smaller fortunes will be in their debt, and in many ways under obligations to them."[41] The notion that material dependency generates oligarchic power had figured prominently in the tradition of republican thought, especially in the work of James Harrington. Harrington had argued that when the gentry class became too rich relative to the republic's small freeholders, the latter class would be rendered dependent upon the former for material sustenance. It was by such a process that one class acquired large numbers of servants and dependents and gained "empire" in the state.[42] Adams drew on Harrington's view in the *Defence* to highlight the influence that accrued to wealth on account of material dependency:

> Riches will hold the first place, in civilized societies, at least, among the principles of power, and will often prevail, not only over all the principles of authority, but over all the advantages of birth, knowledge, and fame. For, as Harrington says, "Men are hung upon riches; not of choice, as upon the other, but of necessity, and by the teeth. Forasmuch as he who wants bread, is his servant that will feed him; and if a man thus feeds a whole people, they are under his empire."[43]

Under conditions of inequality, the have-nots would be induced—whether by gratitude, want, or necessity—to do the will of the haves.

Apart from material dependencies, wealth was also accompanied by extensive social relations. Just as those individuals of illustrious birth were empowered by social connections, the rich would gain influence over "men of letters, men of the learned professions, and others" simply through "acquaintance, conversation, and civilities." And as I will examine in depth in later chapters, he observed that wealth was everywhere accompanied by "a degree of admiration, abstracted from all dependence, obligation, expectation, or even acquaintance" that gave the wealthy influence over their admirers.[44]

If qualities like wealth and birth could be seen to enjoy a great deal of political influence, it seemed important to scrutinize the common republican assumption held by the likes of Franklin and Turgot that republics are necessarily "founded on the equality of all citizens." Indeed, Adams went as far as to write that in every state, even in egalitarian Massachusetts, "there are inequalities which God and nature have planted there, and which no human legislator ever can eradicate." Just as merit was, in practice, the basis for a natural aristocracy, the influence of birth and wealth too were "founded in the constitution of human nature" and constituted a "natural aristocracy among mankind."[45]

The notion of a natural aristocracy of the wealthy and well-born sat oddly within the context of the historical discourse on aristocracy. It was much more common to draw a clear distinction, as Jefferson did, between an undeserving, artificial aristocracy of wealth and birth, on the one hand, and a natural aristocracy of talent and virtue on the other. After all, to describe wealth and birth as constituting a natural aristocracy seemed tantamount to granting moral superiority to the rich and wellborn. Was Adams really suggesting that aristocracy was natural and therefore morally justified? Did he believe that the rich and wellborn were distinguished from the rest of society not just on account of man-made privileges, but also on account of nature or even divine right?

Such questions seemed especially justified when considering Adams's ongoing frustration with the ideas of "natural equality" espoused by his European antagonists. "I have never read reasoning more absurd, sophistry more gross," wrote Adams, "in proof of the Athanasian creed, or transubstantiation, than the subtle labors of Helvetius and Rousseau to demonstrate the natural equality of mankind."[46] Yet if such statements appeared to expose Adams as hopelessly inegalitarian, the truth was not so simple. What Adams meant precisely in calling the idea of natural equality absurd and sophistic is suggested by his marginal notes in Rousseau's *Discourse on Inequality*.[47] Therein Adams objected to Rousseau's contention that the various sources of social inequality—property, beauty, dexterity—were mere artifacts of advanced societies. He denied Rousseau's speculation that the savage felt no preference for one sexual partner over another and that feelings of preference arose only when man first acquired the idea of beauty. "Never was savage insensible to beauty." Even if he would not refuse any single partner, Adams asked, "if several were offered him, of different figures, colors, beauty, would he have no choice?" Even less plausible was Rousseau's contention that the discord caused by preference for beauty occurred only in an advanced social state. "And were there no battles for a female before this improved state? He makes men more stupid than horses or dogs." Nor was it true that human pride was a mere accident of history produced, as Rousseau had argued, by man's first acknowledgment of his superiority to other animals. "He was proud long before," wrote Adams. Indeed, Adams joked, even individual birds, beasts, and fish showed more pride in their behavior than Rousseau's natural man. And Adams rejected Rousseau's claim that it was only at an advanced social state that men gained the respect of their fellows by distinguishing themselves as "the handsomest, the strongest, the most dexterous, the most eloquent." "These are sources of reputation, influence, and dignity," wrote Adams, "which *in every stage of society* surpass merit, in some instances." The esteem men held for one another did not emerge at a particular stage of history but instead was present among "the two first men or women who met." Likewise, Adams rejected Rousseau's argument that ingenuity and the advantages that flowed from it were by-products of an advanced stage of society. Even the feathers and shells Rousseau's natural man used as ornaments must have required labor and study to collect. To Rousseau's contention that the idea of property emerged only with the practice of agriculture, Adams retorted that even "a club, an hatchet of stone, a bow, an arrow was property before land. So was the lion's skin of Hercules." And to Rousseau's claim that agriculture advantaged the strong and dexterous, who could perform more work and who could work more efficiently, Adams insisted that talent was an "eternal source of inequality in many stages of society." Did not the most ingenious work more efficiently before the advent of agriculture and manufacturing? "Ingenuity gave him an advantage in taking fish, fowls, and all sorts of game: so it did in climbing trees for fruit: or excavating a tree rotten at the heart for a house."[48]

Adams's objection to Rousseau's views was not mere quibbling. The fundamental flaw of Rousseau's account of human nature was its hard distinction between man's natural, presocial condition on the one side, and man's artificial, social condition on the other. As Adams put it, Rousseau believed that "the distinction between a natural and an artificial society is groundless. Nature never intended any society. All society is art. Nothing will do but a paradox." By aligning primitive man with nature, and social man with artifice, Rousseau overlooked those aspects of the social condition that could sensibly be called natural. As Adams had argued in his *Defence*, advantages in such qualities as wealth, birth, and beauty had everywhere and always resulted in disproportionate social influence. Rousseau had gone to great lengths to show that many so-called natural inequalities were in fact "merely the results of habit and of the various ways of life adopted by men in society." But if aristocratic influence existed as an empirical regularity across time and space, what difference did it make whether it was social or presocial? As Adams asked: "If inequalities were not natural but only the necessary effect of association, what then?"[49] It made no difference for the design of institutions, and Rousseau, in drawing such a sharp distinction, had led a generation of revolutionaries to overlook the persistent reality of aristocratic power.

The truth that so many of Adams's readers missed is that he was not working within the traditional dichotomy that pitted a natural and morally salutary aristocracy against an artificial and morally dubious one. Indeed, in his description of natural aristocracy, Adams uncoupled the natural from the moral. The inequalities that existed between the wellborn and the rest and between the rich and the poor were "natural" simply in the sense that, in Adams's words, "they have a natural and inevitable influence in society."[50] The rich and the wellborn could be said to constitute a "natural" aristocracy not because the most fortunate were morally superior, but because *influence* could be counted on to accrue to the possessors of wealth and illustrious lineage. Moral judgments aside, Adams thought that aristocracy was natural to politics in much the same way that gravity was natural to physics. Just as an object could be expected to fall toward the center of the Earth, power could be expected to flow with lawlike regularity to the rich and wellborn.

In moral terms, Adams shared the egalitarian tenets of his republican contemporaries. Indeed, he explicitly rejected a certain type of moral inegalitarianism that had often accompanied discussions of natural inequality in the history of political thought. In his *Defence*, Adams prefaced his discussion of natural inequality in America by stating that there was "a moral and political equality of rights and duties among all the individuals." He repudiated the classical idea of natural inequality found, most influentially, in Aristotle's *Politics*. The argument went that certain classes of men—farmers, merchants, and artisans—should not count as citizens because the city is constituted for the purpose of virtue, and men of such classes take no part in virtue but instead pursue only the necessities of life. Such men might serve as "instruments useful to civil life," but they could not be properly counted among the citizenry. Adams denounced Aristotle's argument as "the most unphilosophical, the most inhuman and cruel that can be conceived." There is no doctrine, Adams scoffed, "which goes so far as this towards forfeiting to the human species the character of rational creatures." It was true that farmers, merchants, and mechanics "are too inattentive to public affairs, and too patient under oppression." But this did not mean that such men could not be granted equal rights as citizens to vote and be represented in an assembly. "The meanest understanding is equal to the duty of saying who is the man in his neighborhood whom he most esteems, and loves best, for his knowledge, integrity, and benevolence." Furthermore, the claim that men of the laboring classes were by nature inferior was untrue, and thus could not justify placing limits on opportunities to advance:

> The understandings . . . of husbandmen, merchants, and mechanics, are not always the meanest; there arise, in the course of human life, many among them of the most splendid geniuses, the most active and benevolent dispositions, and most undaunted bravery. The moral equality that nature has unalterably established among men, gives these an undoubted right to have every road opened to them for advancement in life and in power that is open to any others.

Adams wanted institutions that would enable such men to "exert all their faculties, and enjoy all the honors, offices, and commands, both in peace and war, of which they are capable."[51] As we have seen, he did think that persisting inequalities had important implications for social life and for the design of political institutions, but even as he insisted on the political-sociological importance of inequality, he rejected the inegalitarian doctrines that had characterized much of premodern republican thought.

Indeed, Adams fixated on inequalities of wealth and birth not to justify them but instead to warn that they would continue to wreak havoc long after formal inequalities of rank had been abolished. "As long as human nature shall have passions and imagination," it was safe to assume that wealth and birth "will have more influence than reason and equity can justify."[52] The truth was that both Adams and Jefferson drew from a common source when developing their views of aristocracy. Both understood elite power in terms that were heavily influenced by the writings of James Harrington. In Harrington's *Commonwealth of Oceana*, which Adams quotes at length in the *Defence*, the order of men called "the few" was distinguished both by such qualities as wisdom, prudence, and courage, which Harrington called "goods of the mind," and by riches, which Harrington called "the goods of fortune."[53] The aristocracy's dual sources of distinction made it Janus-faced in character. If, as a wealthy, "overbalancing" gentry, the aristocracy could be the bane of popular government, its virtue and wisdom nonetheless made it "the very life and soul of it." The people, wrote Harrington, "have not only a natural but a positive obligation to make use of [them] as their guides."[54] But it was critical that the few not hold power on account of their fortune alone, for although the wisdom of the few "may be the light of mankind . . . the interest of the few is not the profit of mankind, nor of a commonwealth."[55]

Though the two ex-presidents both drew from this notion of natural aristocracy, they appropriated Harrington's ideas in different ways. Jefferson thought that the abolition of hereditary privilege and the establishment of republican institutions had placed America on a path toward a well-ordered republic in which the elite class would be characterized by what Harrington called "the goods of the mind." Adams, by contrast, insisted that it was qualities like wealth and birth—"the goods of fortune"—that would continue to predominate.

Two Votes

During the same stretch of months when Adams exchanged letters with Jefferson on the nature of aristocracy, he received by mail a mysterious document. "I had scarcely sealed my last Letter to you," he wrote to Jefferson, "when they brought me from the Post Office a Packett, without Post Mark, without Letter, without name date or place." The nicely sealed document appeared to be the first installment of a larger work and was titled simply "Aristocracy." Adams went on: "I gravely composed my risible Muscles and read it through. It is, from beginning to End an Attack upon me by name for the doctrines of Aristocracy in my 3 Volumes of 'Defence.'"[56]

Adams suspected, and would soon confirm, that the author was the Virginian planter, politician, and political theorist John Taylor of Caroline. Taylor had arrived on the national political scene as a senator in 1792 amid intensifying controversy over Alexander Hamilton's financial policies. Like Jefferson, he had viewed Hamilton's policies as constituting a scheme of corruption that threatened to undermine the republic, and he had worked tirelessly with Jefferson to build a party capable of resisting Hamilton's designs.

Meanwhile, ever since Taylor first encountered Adams's *Defence*, he had wished to refute it in writing. According to Taylor, Adams had deeply misconstrued the principles of republican government in America, clinging to outmoded ideas of balanced government and the ancient "numerical analysis" of the "the one, the few, and the many" when this entire framework had been supplanted in the modern era by the theory of popular sovereignty.[57] Important to our discussion is that a central part of Taylor's critique was a challenge of Adams's idea of a "natural aristocracy." According to Taylor, Adams had misconstrued the reality of aristocracy in two basic ways. First, Adams had traced aristocracy to nature when in fact all aristocracies throughout history had been *artificial*—not ordained by nature but manufactured by man. In support of this contention, Taylor relayed the history of aristocracy in three stages and argued that at each stage the aristocratic class had been the product of human intrigue. The "aristocracy of the first age," composed of the priestly class, had been "created and supported by superstition." In the second age, an aristocracy of feudal lords was "produced by conquest." In the third and present age, the aristocracy of financial elites had been "erected by paper and patronage." Adams had simply ignored this history of artifice, and in his ignorance he had placed the artificial institution of aristocracy on the false foundation of nature. Just like those confused thinkers who had defended the divine right of kings, Adams had granted an unjustified permanence and moral stature to an institution that was essentially man-made and therefore eradicable.[58]

Furthermore, Taylor argued that insofar as Adams had criticized aristocracy, he had singled out the wrong group of aristocrats. The old aristocracies of priests and feudal barons—those who had predominated in the first two historical ages—had long since declined in political power and importance. A diffusion of literacy had supplanted widespread superstition, which had been the foundation of priestly power. And more recently, the reform of land laws and the rise of commercial enterprise had broken up landed wealth—the chief basis of feudal aristocracy. "Why," Taylor asked, "has Mr. Adams written volumes to instruct us how to manage an order of nobles, sons of the Gods . . . or one of feudal barons, holding great districts of unalienable country, warlike, high spirited, turbulent and dangerous; now that these orders are no more?"[59]

According to Taylor, the true threat originated in the most recent wave of aristocracy. Like Jefferson, Taylor pointed to the complex of emerging financial institutions as the new source of aristocratic domination. Adams, by focusing on forms of aristocracy that had been reduced to historical relics, was "fencing with a shadow," preoccupied with the elites of bygone ages "whilst he passes over in silence the aristocracy of paper and patronage, more numerous, more burdensome, unexposed to public jealousy by the badge of title, and not too honorable or high spirited to use and serve executive power for the sake of pillaging the people."[60]

Adams's reply was defiant. He did not hesitate to point to the irony that Taylor himself was something of an aristocrat, having amassed "a handsome fortune" by marrying the only child of the notable politician John Penn, who had served in the Continental Congress and signed the Declaration of Independence.[61] But most frustrating of all was that Taylor had overlooked the extent to which he and Adams were in agreement in their critiques of aristocracy. Adams did not disagree with Taylor's contention that financiers composed a dangerous elite. "I most assuredly will not controvert this point," he wrote Jefferson upon reading Taylor's text. Indeed, Adams had increasingly set his own critical sights on financial elites. In a recent series of letters to Benjamin Rush, Adams had lamented the emergence of a new moneyed interest generated by the proliferation of banks. He did not oppose banks as such: "They are absolutely and indispensably necessary in the present State of the World. An Attempt to annihilate or prevent them would be as Romantic an Adventure, as any in Don Quixote." But he did support dramatic reform of the banking system: the elimination of all profit-driven banks that issued paper at interest and the establishment of a single national bank with the sole function of holding deposits. Writing to Rush, Adams lamented that the current system of banking had not only made certain individuals rich at the public expense, it had created an "Aristocracy . . . as fatal as the Feudal Barons," with those benefiting from the system constituting "too impregnable a Phalanx to be attacked by any Thing less disciplined than Roman Legions."[62]

Indeed, a few years earlier Adams had observed that a deepened division between creditors and debtors was producing levels of economic inequality and concentrated wealth that called to mind the class conflict of ancient Rome, where there was a

"constant struggle between the rich and the poor," where "speculation and usury kept the state in perpetual broils," where
"patricians lent money at exorbitant interest, and the plebeians were sometimes unable and always unwilling to pay it."
The "spirit of speculation" that had existed in America "from
the days of William Penn, and even long before" had, since the
Revolution, become a "rage" and had laid the foundation for an
immense concentration of wealth in the hands of a few families.
Meanwhile, on the other side of the divide stood "the common
people," a class comprising the debtors and also "the smaller
merchants and shopkeepers, and even the unfortunate and ne-
cessitous who are obliged to fly into the wilderness for a subsistence . . . ." Such a class would naturally feel resentful toward
rising inequalities:

> A farmer or a tradesman, who cannot, by his utmost industry
> and frugality, in a life of seventy years, do more than support
> a moderate family, and lay up four or five thousand dollars,
> must think it very hard when he sees these vast fortunes
> made *per saltum*, these mushrooms growing up in a night.

Adams saw ample reason, in this context, why many would turn
to Jefferson's party for redress. Unlike his Federalist contemporaries who often attributed Jefferson's electoral success to a
turbulent, untrammeled democratic spirit, Adams believed that
the people's embrace of democratic-republican leadership followed from their observation of an elite's unjust accumulation
of wealth. The common people, struck with "grief and jealousy
and resentment," could be expected to turn to leaders whose
professed aim was to oppose the faction responsible for their
hardship.[63]

Yet in spite of the commonalities he shared with the perspectives of Taylor and the Jeffersonians, Adams insisted that Taylor

was deeply confused in his notions of aristocracy. From Adams's perspective, the financial aristocracy that Taylor described was not something distinct or separate from the natural aristocracy of fortune that he had written so much about. Indeed, Adams believed that Taylor had completely misunderstood the concepts of "natural" and "aristocracy" that he had employed in the *Defence*. "Aristocracy," Adams warned, was a word shrouded with ambiguity, "employed to signify any thing, every thing, and nothing." Adams exhorted Taylor not to mistake his idea of natural aristocracy with the classical Greek idea of "the government of the best men." Though one could easily "produce a hundred authorities" in support of the classical conception, "this would all be waste water." According to Adams's reading of history, the aristocratic class had no special claim to ethical superiority. "Despots, monarchs, aristocrats, and democrats have, in all ages hit, at times, upon the best men, in the best sense of the word." Meanwhile, aristocracies were like all other governing systems in having often granted power to "the very worst men; the men who have the most devotedly and the most slavishly flattered their vanity, gratified their most extravagant passions, and promoted their selfish and private views." Moreover, moral superiority was simply too nebulous an idea to distinguish men from one another with any reliability. "Who is to make the selection," Adams asked, "of the best men from the second best?"[64]

It was not moral superiority that distinguished aristocrats but instead "superiorities of influence."[65] When it came time to present a simple definition of the word "aristocracy," it was clear that the concept of "influence" was the essence of Adams's definition:

Without searching volumes, Mr. Taylor, I will tell you in a few words what I mean by an aristocrat, and, consequently, what I mean by aristocracy. By an aristocrat, I mean every man who can command or influence two votes; one besides his own.

To designate a man an aristocrat, one need not know whether he is virtuous or vicious, talented or average, but only whether he could reliably procure additional support for his causes. An aristocrat was simply "a citizen who can command or govern two votes or more in society."[66]

This definition of aristocracy must have struck Taylor as so broad and all-encompassing as to be meaningless.[67] As if to undermine his own efforts to narrow and define the meaning of aristocracy, Adams proceeded in his letters to Taylor to intimate that *any* distinguishing quality could garner "votes" and thereby designate an individual an aristocrat. Virtue, talent, learning, wealth, or birth could make an aristocrat, and so could face, figure, eloquence, and intrigue. Also counted among the sources of aristocracy were qualities opposite in every other way: loquacity and taciturnity, frankness and reserve, deism and atheism—all could be sources of aristocratic influence.[68]

And yet, as Adams continued his correspondence with Taylor, it became clear that the chief sources of aristocracy were the ones he had emphasized in his earlier writings: birth and wealth. Adams insisted to Taylor that these two aristocratic qualities worked to reinforce one another. The rich could well afford to erect "durable, costly, and permanent memorials" to ancestors, thereby distinguishing their own family lineage from all those ordinary families whose descendants "lie mingled with the dust, totally forgotten."[69]

Regarding the aristocratic power of wealth, Adams repeated his earlier contention that inequalities of property create relations of dependency between the haves and the have-nots. He pressed Taylor to imagine a man owning one hundred thousand acres of land with one thousand families settled on the land as tenants. If he is a "humane, easy, generous" landlord, he will acquire influence with his tenants on account of their gratitude. They will feel attached to him and inclined to think as he thinks and vote as he votes. And if he is instead "an austere, griping, racking, rack-renting tyrant," his tenants will fear offending him and will at least "pretend to think with him, and vote as he would have them." By his wealth, the landlord becomes an aristocrat as long as he "can obtain by gratitude or fear only one vote more than his own from his tenants."[70]

The aristocratic quality of wealth could be called natural because influence accrued to the wealthy with lawlike regularity. For Adams, there was a great deal at stake in conveying this point. Jeffersonians like Taylor insisted that insofar as there existed an oligarchic elite in America, it was one of an essentially artificial kind. Aristocracy was understood as man-made and therefore changeable by man. As we have seen, Jefferson accepted that the rich and wellborn continued to constitute a *pseudo* aristocracy, but he insisted that in a modern republic the only *natural* aristocracy was one made up of talent, virtue, and other meritorious qualities.

To Adams's mind, the clear-cut Jeffersonian distinction between the natural and pseudo aristoi would not stand. He agreed that the power of wealth and birth—what Harrington had called "the goods of fortune"—was not morally legitimate. But to call that power artificial was to underestimate its resilience. To Jefferson's efforts to elevate the goods of the mind over the goods of fortune, Adams responded that "birth and wealth together have prevailed over virtue and talents in all ages." He quipped that even Hercules had failed to subdue the powers of birth and wealth. If Jefferson dared to deny the natural power of the goods of fortune, Adams promised to provide "examples drawn from your own Virginia, and from every other State in the Union, and from the history of every nation, civilized and savage, from all we know of the time of the creation of the world."[71]

FORTUNE, MERIT, AND REFORM

Adams believed that the natural aristocracy of fortune would persist in spite of republican reform efforts. He doubted the possibility, suggested most adamantly by Madison, that aristocrats could be controlled through the mechanics of elections. "Will it be pretended, that the jealousy and vigilance of the people, and their power to discard them at the next election, will restrain them?" The assumption that the vigilance of the electorate would constrain oligarchic elites rested on the expectation that the people would be deferential one moment and vigilant the next; but this was a contradictory assumption:

> It is a contradiction to suppose that a body of electors should have at one moment a warm affection and entire confidence in a man, so as to intrust him with authority, limited or unlimited, over their lives and fortunes; and the next moment after his election, to commence a suspicion of him, that shall prompt them to watch all his words, actions, and motions, and dispose them to renounce and punish him.[72]

Contrary to the view of elections that would be embraced by the likes of Madison and by many twentieth-century political scientists, Adams doubted that the people in their electoral capacity would reliably set aside their admiration and affection for their elected representatives in order to hold corrupt officials accountable.

Nor did Adams concur with Madison's prediction that elections would mitigate the aristocratic threat by elevating the *best* men to office. In his *Defence*, Adams scrutinized a selection scheme found in David Hume's *Idea of a Perfect Commonwealth*, a text that likely influenced Madison's views of electoral selection. Hume had recommended a complex scheme of senatorial government whereby a popular vote elected ten thousand county-level representatives, who in turn elected eleven hundred magistrates, who in turn elected a powerful body of senators. Such a design, while assuring that the chief magistrates of the commonwealth would be dependent on the people, would also increase the likelihood that those responsible for the final selection were "men of fortune and education" and not "an undistinguishing rabble."[73] Madison probably drew inspiration from Hume's design when sketching out his original plan for the federal constitution.[74] Adams, in contrast, characterized Hume's system as "a complicated aristocracy" that would "soon behave like all other aristocracies." The elite few, however carefully selected, would nonetheless be allowed to manage the executive power. Moreover, without popular representatives in the highest level of government, ruling elites would be guarded from "the eyes of the people."[75]

If schemes of electoral design would not solve the problem, Adams was likewise skeptical of the Jeffersonian vision for political education. Adams never shared the classical republican faith in education as a solution to the problem of oligarchy. Like Jefferson, he had long embraced the diffusion of education as a worthwhile enterprise of the state. He praised Charondas, an ancient lawgiver of Catania, for ordaining that "all the sons of every family should learn to write and read, under masters in the pay of the public"—an act that alone "has merit enough to consecrate to immortality the memory of this legislator, and deserves to be imitated, at least by every free people."[76] He rejected the thesis he attributed to Rousseau that "knowledge is corruption;

that arts, sciences, and taste have deformed the beauty and destroyed the felicity of human nature." Knowledge, he thought, tended to promote happiness, and he urged those with means to establish schools and universities and to "employ every means and opportunity to spread information, even to the lowest dregs of the people."[77] But whatever the value of general education, Adams held out little hope for education to improve the judgment of the electorate. Educated or not, mankind had tended throughout history to prefer in their choices the rich and the wellborn over the meritorious. Even philosophers—those most committed in principle to the goods of the mind—tended in practice to value the goods of fortune, so much so that "in marrying their children, [they] prefer the rich, the handsome, and the well-descended, to the wise and good."[78]

Adams likewise rejected the classical republican project of using education to mold a virtuous class of leaders. As he had written in the *Defence*, ancient writers believed that a well-ordered republic required that citizens be trained "to regard the great duties of life . . . and the esteem of their fellow-citizens, as the principal source of their enjoyment."[79] Such an education regime may have been plausible, wrote Adams, in "small communities, especially where the slaves were many, and the citizens few." But in a large nation burdened with bringing up millions "whom no principles, no sentiments derived from education, can restrain from trampling on the laws," schooling could never achieve the desired end. Adams did not disagree entirely with the Jeffersonian idea that education would give rise to aristocracy. Graduates of Harvard, after all, had constituted an aristocracy throughout the history of Massachusetts:

These men, in schools, academies, colleges, and universities; these men, in the shape of ministers, lawyers, and

physicians; these men, in academies of arts and sciences, in
agricultural societies, in historical societies, in medical societies and in antiquarian societies, in banking institutions
and in Washington benevolent societies, govern the state.[80]

But Adams rejected the notion that the educated elite would
be uniquely virtuous or trustworthy. Knowledge, after all,
was available to "knaves and hypocrites . . . as well as honest, candid, and sincere men." Knowledge, Adams insisted, "is
employed as an engine and a vehicle to propagate error and
falsehood, treason and vice, as well as truth, honor, virtue, and
patriotism."[81]

Perhaps most important of all from Adams's point of view,
Jefferson made a fundamental mistake in his failure to recognize the grip that great fortunes had acquired on the minds of
the American citizenry, especially in an era when new commercial aristocracies were continually emerging, "springing up
in this Country not from Virtues and Talents so much as from
Banks and Land Jobbing." He referred Jefferson to the recent
episode involving the rich and well-born Madame Bowdoin
in which, in response to her remarriage following the death of
her husband, "a violent Alarm was excited and spread in Boston and through the country."[82] The public had taken a deep
interest in the affair and had viewed it as a matter of personal
concern. Considering that "an hundred other foreign Aristocracies have sown and are sowing their Seeds in this Country,"
the episode was likely to be repeated.[83]

Under such conditions, to think that the most talented and
virtuous would rise to prominence was dangerously naïve. Adams
relayed to Jefferson the lament of Samuel Johnson: "One truth
is clear, by all the world confessed, Slow rises worth, by poverty
depressed."[84] Merit would enjoy no special privilege in the new
republic. To the contrary, as long as wealth and birth retained its

influence, the idealization of talent could only serve to cloak the reality of oligarchic power. "Fashion has introduced an indeterminate Use of the Word 'Talents,'" wrote Adams. If talents were what distinguished America's ruling class, then such sources of influence as "Education, Wealth, Strength, Air, Complexion, Physiognomy" should all be called "talents." Was it an inequality of talents, he facetiously asked Jefferson, that accounted for the emerging aristocracy of bankers and speculators? "What Inequality of Talents will be produced by these Land Jobbers? . . . What Inequalities of Talent, have been introduced into this Country by these Aristocratical Banks!"[85]

If both Adams and Jefferson employed Harrington's distinction between the goods of the mind and the goods of fortune, Adams never drew a sharp distinction between an aristocracy of fortune and an aristocracy of the mind. He lacked Jefferson's confident belief that the gentry of fortune could be filtered out of power through various reforms and that republican institutions could be relied upon to elevate a natural aristoi of the mind. In contrast, Adams believed that the "goods of fortune" went far beyond mere landed wealth. The rich, after all, would always have greater access to education and therefore intellectual abilities would be mingled with wealth. Virtue and birth were even harder to disentangle. Adams reminded Jefferson that such words as "gentleman" and "generosity"—words so often associated with the virtuous—in fact traced back to the Latin *generosus* and the Greek *eugenic*, roots meaning "not of mean birth" and "born of a noble race."[86]

Jefferson thought that once the material foundations of traditional aristocracy had been eliminated—once hereditary landed wealth had been broken up—what remained of the oligarchic malady could be purged from the political system by means of education and elections. From Adams's point of view, Jefferson was blind to the severity of the problem. The threat of oligarchy could not be pinned on a few pseudo aristocrats or on a few corrupt institutions. A natural aristocracy of fortune had thrived under every form of constitution and would survive the democratic revolution intact. From Adams's perspective, Jefferson and Taylor failed to understand this because they believed that the power of fortune was a product of human artifice, when in fact it was a feature of human nature. As we will see, Adams traced the power of fortune to deep-rooted sentiments—sentiments that would only grow stronger in the wake of the democratic revolution.

CHAPTER THREE

Sympathy for the Rich

The qualities of fortune, such as birth, riches, and
honors, though a man has less reason to esteem
himself for these than for those of his mind or
body, are everywhere acknowledged to glitter with
the brightest lustre in the eyes of the world.

—JOHN ADAMS, *Discourses on Davila*

IN THE PREVIOUS CHAPTERS I have sought to reveal Adams's preoccupation with the threat that oligarchy posed to the new republic. A social and economic elite—what Adams called a natural aristocracy—would continue to wield immense power despite the prohibition of formal aristocratic status and despite dreams of an egalitarian citizenry that would defer only to talent and virtue. What James Harrington had called the goods of fortune would continue to predominate. The wellborn and, even more so, the rich, would continue to enjoy oligarchic influence in America.

What was it that made the qualities of fortune, wealth in particular, politically powerful? It is not self-evident, after all, that advantages in the social and economic realms translate into political power. Observing Jacksonian America, the young French aristocrat Alexis de Tocqueville found that wealth was less a guarantor of political influence than an obstacle to it. "In our day," wrote Tocqueville, "one can say that in the United States the wealthy classes of society are almost entirely out of political affairs and that wealth, far from being a right [to power], is a real cause of disfavor and an obstacle to coming to power." America's democratic culture seemed to condition the rich in peculiar ways. Tocqueville was struck by the humility of the rich American man who could be seen in the middle of the street shaking hands with his shoemaker and casually discussing state affairs. It was not that men had ceased to amass great fortunes. On the contrary, Tocqueville observed that he knew of no country "where the love of money holds a larger place in the heart of man and where they profess a more profound scorn for the theory of the permanent equality of goods." But if Americans were willing to tolerate concentrations of material wealth, the rich were nonetheless denied any special share of social or political influence.[1]

The twentieth-century political scientist Robert Dahl drew a similar conclusion in his landmark study of political power in the city of New Haven, Connecticut. Equality in the political realm could survive alongside vast inequality in the economic realm, Dahl argued, because the resources in different domains were not necessarily *cumulative*. One who is better off in terms of wealth is not by necessity better off in terms of the various educational, religious, and social sources of influence. It was true that in the early years of the republic New Haven's politics had been dominated by a Federalist oligarchy that combined wealth with preeminence in education and social standing. But by the twentieth century, the city had become *pluralistic* in the sense that the economic elite was simply one among many interest groups competing to influence the political agenda.[2]

Adams's understanding of fortune and political power would seem to contradict the Tocquevillian and pluralist views. The question that remains to be addressed is how, precisely, did Adams understand wealth to translate into political influence?

Using Adams's terms, how was it that the rich man commanded two votes, one besides his own?

If there is a single prevailing theory among today's political scientists and commentators, it is that the rich in various ways are able to *buy* influence by bringing unrivaled resources to bear on elections and lobbying efforts. The rich purchase electoral voice through powerful opinion-shaping institutions.[3] They incline representatives to vote their way through well-funded, well-organized lobbying efforts.[4] The wealthiest Americans are able to defeat adverse tax policies through the use of lawyers, accountants, and wealth-management consultants.[5] Adams, too, pointed out the extent to which the rich were able to purchase political influence. It was "a natural and unchangeable inconvenience in all popular elections . . . that he who has the deepest purse, or the fewest scruples about using it, will generally prevail."[6] But Adams also traced the political influence of wealth to a quite different source. It was not just the ability of the rich to buy influence, but also the sentiments of sympathy and admiration for the rich among the people that tended to concentrate influence in the hands of the wealthy. In this respect, Adams subscribed to an older style of political theory that understood political arrangements as based on *psychological* as well as material foundations. Since the origins of Western political philosophy in ancient Athens, analysts of politics had categorized political regimes in relation to the reigning psychological disposition of the citizenry. "Do you know," Socrates asked in the *Republic*,

> that it is necessary that there also be as many forms of human characters as there are forms of regimes? Or do you suppose that the regimes arise "from an oak or rocks" and not from the dispositions of the men in the cities, which, tipping the scale as it were, draw the rest along with them?

Socrates suggested that the regime called oligarchy, which "gets its rulers on the basis of a property assessment," did not arise merely from relations of material dependency, but also from the distinctive psyche of the "oligarchic man"—the man who, frightened by the prospect of misfortune and poverty, "thrusts love of honor and spiritedness headlong out of the throne of his soul" and "turns greedily to money-making." Such a disposition, when widespread, displaced virtue in cities and rendered them oligarchical, for "when wealth and the wealthy are honored in a city, virtue and the good men are less honorable" and "what happens to be honored is practiced, and what is without honor is neglected."[7]

Quite similarly, several major thinkers associated with the eighteenth-century Scottish Enlightenment understood political power to derive from something other than brute material force. "NOTHING appears more surprizing to those, who consider human affairs with a philosophical eye," wrote David Hume, "than the easiness with which the many are governed by the few." Force was naturally "always on the side of the governed" and therefore could not account for the power of the governors. Rather, it was "*on opinion* only that government is founded." And moreover, the opinion that bestowed authority on the few was not merely "opinion of interest"—or "the sense of the general advantage which is reaped from government"—but also the "opinion of right," including a sentiment of the "right to power" that Hume associated with "the attachment which all nations have to their ancient government."[8]

As we will see, John Adams was a careful student of the Scottish Enlightenment. More than any other Founding Era American, he engaged with the long tradition of thought that emphasized the psychological bases of social and political power. The fruit of his efforts was the series of essays entitled *Discourses on Davila*, a work that Adams would describe as the fourth and final volume of his *Defence.*[9] It is to the *Discourses* that we now turn.

DISCOURSES ON DAVILA

"It is . . . uncommonly interesting to picture a busy and influential political figure, in a difficult and highly controversial period of our history . . . sitting down to do a little psychologizing for himself."[10] This is how Arthur O. Lovejoy described the anomaly of *Discourses on Davila*, a work of subtle moral psychology that John Adams wrote amid his turbulent term as America's first vice president. Adams felt moved by recent events to revisit and rearticulate his political convictions. For one, his basic commitment to republicanism had been called into question when, in his constitutional role as president of the Senate, he injected himself into a heated debate that preoccupied the Senate for most of its first month. Wishing to grant the presidential office a level of dignity commensurate with its importance, Adams supported the title "His Highness the President of the United States of America and Protector of the Rights of the Same."[11] In the end the cause was defeated when the House and Senate together opted for the simpler "President of the United States." The episode added considerable weight to suspicions that Adams harbored monarchical sympathies.[12]

More recently, he had been agitated by news of revolution in France. The course of events, widely cheered in America, left Adams conflicted. Writing to his friend Richard Price, the British moral philosopher and preacher who had delivered influential sermons in support of the revolutionary cause, he affirmed that he shared the sentiments and principles underlying the upheaval. But if the French revolutionaries were similar to the Americans in their "general sentiments," they were morally and constitutionally entering uncharted territory by placing the entire sovereignty of a vast republic in a single assembly. "I have learned by awful experience," wrote Adams, "to rejoice with trembling."[13]

The *Discourses on Davila* first appeared as a series of letters in the *Gazette of the United States*, a Federalist semiweekly, with the first letter appearing on 27 April 1790. Adams ostensibly set out to provide a translation and commentary on Enrico Caterino Davila's *Historia delle guerre civili di Francia*. The Italian historian's account of the rivalries and upheavals of sixteenth-century France, Adams suggested, had much to teach the present. But the richest portion of the work had little to do with Davila's *Historia*. At the end of the first letter Adams signaled a change of topic. "Before we proceed in our discourses," he wrote, "it will assist us . . . to turn our thoughts for a few moments to the constitution of the human mind." For fourteen of the thirty-two letters, Adams focused not on the convulsions of sixteenth-century France but on the subtleties of the human psyche. He drew on works as various as Alexander Pope's *Essay on Man* and Shakespeare's *Tempest* to explore the nature of avarice, ambition, and emulation.

Adams had long harbored an interest in the subtleties of moral psychology. Arthur Lovejoy, in his study of eighteenth-century conceptions of human nature, remarked that Adams participated more than any other American in his era's rich discourses on moral and social psychology: "Adams may be said . . . to have been the most assiduous American student of 'social psychology' in the eighteenth century."[14] One of Adams's first public writings, published in the *Boston Gazette* in 1763, was an essay exploring man's capacity for self-deceit. With an intricacy that anticipated the *Discourses*, he described our troubling tendency to trick ourselves into thinking our actions are morally motivated when in fact they spring from self-regarding desires. Moved by self-love and caught in "swarms of passions," we are "prone to mistake the impulses of these for the dictates of our consciences."[15]

Scholars have noted that Adam Smith's *Theory of Moral Sentiments* loomed especially large in Adams's analysis. In fact, large sections of the *Discourses* consist of mere quotations and paraphrases of Smith's text, a feature that has led some to dismiss the work as merely derivative. Yet, when understood in the context of his larger body of political writings, the series of essays stands as a remarkably original work. As C. Wright Mills observed upon analyzing the *Discourses*, Adams's originality lies in the facility with which he related the phenomena of social life to the problems of political power.[16] It is true that the *Discourses* was largely an effort to digest the social-psychological insights of the Scottish Enlightenment, but what to the Scots had been a subtle theory of moral psychology became, in Adams's mind, a unique conception of oligarchic power.[17]

SYMPATHY AND DISTINCTION

As we will see, John Adams thought that widespread sympathy for the rich could be a potent source of power for social and economic elites. If this strikes readers as an odd proposition, it is perhaps because sympathy is a concept more often associated with the plight of the poor and downtrodden than with the predicament of the rich and distinguished. Likewise, insofar as sympathy is associated with political power, it is more easily understood as empowering the causes of the disadvantaged and marginalized. To give one prominent example, American abolitionists appealed to public sympathy to mobilize support for the antislavery cause. By moving beyond appeals to self-interest and attempting to kindle the fellow feeling of free Americans for the suffering endured by slaves, they sought to harness the power of sympathy on behalf of the disempowered.[18]

Yet, if sympathy is more easily understood as a sentiment working to empower efforts on behalf of the downtrodden, Scottish historians and moralists of the eighteenth century repeatedly described the same sentiment as a source of power for the rich and distinguished. Though perhaps "improperly in the eye of a strict moralist," according to the historian and political philosopher John Millar, wealth "seldom fails to procure a degree of admiration and respect." Millar described the attraction to wealth among the people at length:

> The poor are attracted and dazzled by the apparent happiness and splendor of the rich; and they regard a man of large fortune with a sort of wonder, and partial prepossession, which disposes them to magnify and overrate all his advantages. If they are so far beneath him as not to be soured by the malignity of envy, they behold with pleasure and satisfaction the sumptuousness of his table, the magnificence of his equipage, the facility and quickness with which he is whirled from place to place, the number of his attendants, the readiness with which they observe all his movements, and run to promote his wishes.[19]

Similarly, the Scottish historian and moral philosopher Adam Ferguson highlighted the tendency among the people in commercial societies to bestow admiration and influence on fortune rather than character. Though we "think we are talking of men," wrote Ferguson, "we are boasting of their estates, their dress, and their palaces." With full knowledge that the object of our admiration is merely "a pageant in the midst of his fortune," we nonetheless follow him, and "look up with an envious, servile, or dejected mind, to what is, in itself, scarcely fit to amuse children."[20]

Furthermore, it was observed that sentiments like admiration and sympathy were sources of social power. Millar observed that sympathy motivated the people to follow the rich in their pursuits:

> Delighted with a situation which appears to them so agreeable, and catching from each other the contagion of sympathetic feelings, they are often prompted by an enthusiastic fervor, to exalt his dignity to promote his enjoyments, and to favour his pursuits.

It was true that the authority of the rich was "chiefly supported by selfish considerations," because the rich man provided "employment, and consequently subsistence to many individuals" who, in turn, "have more or less an interest in paying him respect and submission." But it was the "splendor" of wealth and not just the dependency it generated that explained its power.[21]

The most vivid and detailed account of sympathy as a source of elite power was developed by Adam Smith in his *Theory of Moral Sentiments*. Smith recognized that the word "sympathy" was most often associated with fellow feeling for those experiencing sorrow and suffering. But he insisted nonetheless that human beings more readily sympathize with the joy of the successful than with the sorrow and suffering of the downtrodden. "Our sympathy with sorrow . . . has been more taken notice of than our sympathy with joy." But this, Smith insisted, was a mere "prejudice" that covered over the reality that "our propensity to sympathize with joy is much stronger than our propensity to sympathize with sorrow." The reason for this tendency had to do with the difficulty of entering into a state of fellow feeling with the least fortunate. We find it easy to sympathize with success, because even the greatest success does not alter a man's happiness in any large degree. "What can be added to the happiness of a man who is in health, who is out of debt, and has a clear conscience? . . . Between this condition and the highest pitch of human prosperity, the interval is but a trifle." But if success does not drastically alter our happiness, the same could not be said of misfortune. If the difference success makes is slight, the gap between the average state of happiness and the lowest depths of sorrow is "immense and prodigious." As Smith put it, misfortune "necessarily depresses the mind of the sufferer much more below its natural state, than prosperity can elevate him above it." This means that in order to sympathize with sorrow, one "must depart much further from his own natural and ordinary temper of mind." The result is that, upon hearing of another's joy, "our heart abandons itself with satisfaction." In contrast, "it is painful to go along with grief, and we always enter into it with reluctance."[22]

Smith described in unsettling detail the effects of our selective sympathy. The successful man expects to be sympathized with and therefore "does not fear . . . to announce himself with shouts of exultation." The downtrodden man, by contrast, hides his sorrows in anticipation of a cold reception:

> The wretch whose misfortunes call upon our compassion feels with what reluctance we are likely to enter into his sorrow, and therefore proposes his grief to us with fear and hesitation: he even smothers the half of it, and is ashamed, upon account of this hard-heartedness of mankind, to give vent to the fulness of his affliction.

It was a striking discrepancy of fellow feeling. "How hearty are the acclamations of the mob . . . at a triumph or a public entry? And how sedate and moderate is commonly their grief at an execution?"[23]

According to Smith, the human propensity to sympathize with joy meant, in practice, that human beings tend to sympathize with the most socially distinguished. One might think that a tendency to sympathize with the happiest would mean widespread sympathy for the wisest and most virtuous, but the truth, Smith insisted, is that "the real and steady admirers of wisdom and virtue" are small in number. "We frequently see the respectful attentions of the world more strongly directed towards the rich and the great, than towards the wise and the virtuous." Most of us consider "the great"—those set apart by rank or some other kind of social distinction—to be the happiest among us. To be distinguished and recognized by others is "the very state which, in all our waking dreams and idle reveries, we had sketched out to ourselves as the final object of all our desires." When we consider the way of life of the most distinguished individuals, "it seems to be almost the abstract idea of a perfect and happy state." We therefore cannot help but sympathize with the most distinguished and make their cares and concerns our own. "The man of rank and distinction . . . is observed by all the world," wrote Smith. "Every body is eager to look at him, and to conceive, at least by sympathy, that joy and exultation with which his circumstances naturally inspire him."[24]

Smith did not approve of this tendency. In no uncertain terms, he condemned man's propensity to sympathize with the most distinguished, calling it "the great and most universal cause of the corruption of our moral sentiments." Smith did believe that the deferential tendency was valuable insofar as it created and maintained an orderly society, but the moral cost was undeniable. It made for a society desensitized to the preoccupations and pains of the least fortunate, so much so that if a "stranger to human nature" could see the indignation we show toward the misfortunes of our superiors alongside our indifference to the miseries of those below us, he would conclude "that pain must be more agonizing, and the convulsions of death more terrible, to persons of higher rank than to those of meaner stations."[25]

Smith wrote of the sympathy felt for kings that "every calamity that befalls them, every injury that is done them, excites in the breast of the spectator ten times more compassion and resentment than he would have felt, had the same things happened to other men." It was such sympathy that made kings and their misfortunes the subjects for tragedies in the theater. "The traitor who conspires against the life of his monarch," wrote Smith, "is thought a greater monster than any other murderer." And important for our discussion, Smith counted "the rich" as among that distinguished class that receives the most sympathy and admiration. For him, it was sympathy for the rich that explained the puzzling tendency of men in commercial societies to toil and strive for riches. It could not simply be for convenience that we pursue wealth, considering that our basic necessities are easily supplied by even "the wages of the meanest labourer." If we toil to get rich, we do so because we know that wealth is "observed . . . attended to . . . taken notice of with sympathy, complacency, and approbation."[26] Along with his Scottish Enlightenment contemporaries, Smith suggested that in the commercial republics of the future, wealth would glitter with the same luster as royalty. As we will see, it was the concept of sympathy for the rich that John Adams found especially useful in his efforts to comprehend the oligarchic tendencies of early America.

WEALTH AND DISTINCTION IN AMERICA

John Adams shared with Adam Smith the view that human beings are universally moved by "the passion for distinction," a desire "to be observed, considered, esteemed, praised, beloved, and admired" by others. Adams insisted that every human being, "whether they be old or young, rich or poor, high or low, wise or foolish, ignorant or learned . . . is seen to be strongly actuated by a desire to be seen, heard, talked of, approved and respected, by the people about him, and within his knowledge." And just as we long for the consideration of others, we abhor being neglected or overlooked, especially when the consideration denied us is given to another. "In proportion to our affection for the notice of others," wrote Adams, "is our aversion to their neglect." And in proportion to a man's desire to surpass his fellows in the consideration paid him, "he feels a keener affliction when he sees that one or more of them, are more respected than himself."[27]

To put Adams's view in more contemporary terms, it is not utilitarian pleasure-seeking or a Nietzschean will to dominate that most often motivates us, but something closer to what Martin Luther King Jr. called "the drum major instinct," a desire "to be out front . . . to lead the parade . . . to be first."[28] According to Adams, the desire for distinction was a longing endowed in man by nature in order to entice human beings to social virtue. Because mere benevolence, "affection for the good of others," was not sufficient to counter selfishness, it was necessary to sanction mankind with rewards and punishments capable of spurring men "to constant exertions of beneficence." Anticipating the rewards of esteem and admiration, and seeking to avoid the punishments of neglect and contempt, men might "produce something which shall contribute to the comfort, convenience, pleasure, profit, or utility of some or other of the species." They might be made, "by their own vanity, slaves to mankind."[29]

Yet, if the natural function of emulation was to spur men to beneficence, it was not just in good works that the passion was

manifest. Ambition, jealousy, envy, and vanity were all modifi-
cations of the same desire for distinction. And while that desire
could be regulated and directed toward such beneficial ends as
the strengthening of moral and intellectual qualities or the pursuit of various honors and public offices, Adams believed that
the vast majority viewed wealth and other goods of fortune as
the surest signs of distinction.[30] It was true that there were small
numbers for whom the passion for distinction was "refined by
the purest moral sentiments" and who sought admiration and esteem through heroic virtue. It was likewise true that there were
some who sought consideration by crimes and vices. But most
people sought distinction "neither by vices nor virtues; but by the
means which common sense and every day's experience show,
are most sure to obtain it; by riches, by family records, by play,
and other frivolous personal accomplishments."[31] Indeed, qualities of fortune were more esteemed even than those qualities of
mind and body most necessary for personal happiness:

> The intellectual and moral qualities are most within our power,
> and undoubtedly the most essential to our happiness. The
> personal qualities of health, strength, and agility, are next
> in importance. Yet the qualities of fortune, such as birth,
> riches, and honors, though a man has less reason to esteem
> himself for these than for those of his mind or body, are ev-
> erywhere acknowledged to glitter with the brightest lustre
> in the eyes of the world.[32]

For most, therefore, the surest route to distinction was to acquire the qualities of fortune that commanded the most attention.
   Adams was at pains to point out that men sought the goods
of fortune not for their utility but for the consideration that
accompanied them. After all, there was no immediate value in
belonging to a family of illustrious descent. It was true that one

born of a notable family could be assumed to have advantages of education, but these advantages, Adams wrote, derived chiefly from the mother and father, not from family lineage. What did it matter, then, "whether the family is twenty generations upon record, or only two?" The answer was that illustrious names attracted the notice of the world. "Benevolence, sympathy, congratulation, have been so long associated to those names in the minds of the people," he wrote, that such names were "national habits." The pride men showed for illustrious descent was "as irrational and contemptible as the pride of riches." But for all its shamefulness, such pride was no less real, and the craftiest would continue to satisfy it:

> A wise man will lament that any other distinction than that of merit should be made. A good man will neither be proud nor vain of his birth, but will earnestly improve every advantage he has for the public good. A cunning man will carefully conceal his pride; but will indulge it in secret the more effectually, and improve his advantage to greater profit.

The consideration afforded by illustrious descent meant that men would continue to seek distinction by embracing their own lineage and, when possible, by adding prestige to their own family names.[33]

Adams's discussion of man's desire for the goods of fortune ends with a lengthy consideration of the desire for riches that closely resembles Adam Smith's discussion of the same theme in the *Theory of Moral Sentiments*.[34] "Why do men pursue riches? What is the end of avarice?" As with the pursuit of illustrious lineage, Adams found the quest for wealth inexplicable in terms of pleasure maximization. "The labor and anxiety, the enterprises and adventures, that are voluntarily undertaken in pursuit of gain, are out of all proportion to the utility, convenience, or pleasure of riches," observed Adams. A limited daily toil was enough to supply the basic necessities of food, clothes, and shelter. And moreover, the body was in some ways healthier without the consumption of luxuries. Why then, he asked, "are any mortals averse to the situation of the farmer, mechanic, or laborer?"

> Why do we tempt the seas and encompass the globe? Why do any men affront heaven and earth to accumulate wealth, which will forever be useless to them? Why do we make an ostentatious display of riches? Why should any man be proud of his purse, houses, lands, or gardens? or, in better words, why should the rich man glory in his riches? What connection can there be between wealth and pride?[35]

The answer was that riches, like beauty and birth, attracted "the attention, consideration, and congratulations of mankind." Adams described in vivid detail the passions of emulation activated by wealth:

> Riches force the opinion on a man that he is the object of the congratulations of others, and he feels that they attract the complaisance of the public. His senses all inform him, that his neighbors have a natural disposition to harmonize with all those pleasing emotions and agreeable sensations, which the elegant accommodations around him are supposed to excite. . . . His imagination expands, and his heart dilates at these charming illusions. His attachment to his possessions increases as fast as his desire to accumulate more.[36]

Men's hearts dilated at the thought of wealth out of a desire for distinction and not "for the purposes of beneficence or utility." In the modern, commercial republic, this emulative passion affected not just the rich but the broader population, as the equality of free institutions gave rise to material envy. Adams had described this dynamic in the *Defence*: "A citizen perceives his fellow-citizen, whom he holds his equal, [to] have a better coat or hat, a better house or horse, than himself, and sees his neighbors are struck with it, talk of it, and respect him for it. He cannot bear it; he must and will be upon a level with him."[37]

The desire for money as a marker of distinction could also be demonstrated by reference to the suffering of the poor. The poor man suffered less from the lack of material necessities than from the pain of obscurity:

> He feels himself out of the sight of others, groping in the dark. Mankind take no notice of him. He rambles and wanders unheeded. In the midst of a crowd, at church, in the market, at a play, at an execution, or coronation, he is in as much obscurity as he would be in a garret or a cellar. He is not disapproved, censured, or reproached; *he is only not seen.* This total inattention is to him mortifying, painful, and cruel.

The agony of obscurity was so severe that even those of the lowest social station—even common thieves—"court a set of admirers, and plume themselves upon that superiority which they have, or fancy they have, over some others." Even the man with nothing to attract the eyes of his fellows, the one "who is the last and lowest of the human species," seeks recognition from his dog. In a vivid illustration of the natural human aversion to obscurity, Adams relayed the story of such a man insisting on feeding his dog even as he himself starved to death. In reply to a passer-by who advised him to kill or sell the dog, the man refused, replying, "Who will love me then?"[38]

The pursuit of wealth, then, was driven by a raging passion for distinction and a frantic fear of obscurity. This description

of the passion for wealth, it should be noted, was remarkably different than the conception of economic "interest" being developed by Adams's eighteenth-century contemporaries.
As Albert O. Hirschman would later observe, an eighteenth-
century school of moral philosophy that included Francis
Hutcheson, Lord Shaftesbury, and David Hume drew a sharp
distinction between violent, inconstant "passions" on the one
hand, and predictable and relatively harmless "interests" on the
other. The desire for riches was a calm, calculative desire, characterized by a "willingness to pay high costs to achieve even
higher benefits."[39] The rational quality of the love of gain set it
apart from those wild and dangerous passions that had inspired
aristocrats to strive for honor and glory. The desire for riches
was not a passion but a mere "interest" and was therefore essentially innocuous. "There are few ways in which man can be
more innocently employed," wrote Samuel Johnson, "than in
getting money."[40] Adams, by contrast, grouped the love of gain
alongside ambition and the love of praise as an "aristocratical"
passion that was unlimited in its nature:

> The love of gold grows faster than the heap of acquisition;
> the love of praise increases by every gratification, till it stings
> like an adder, and bites like a serpent; till the man is mis-
> erable every moment when he does not snuff the incense.
> Ambition strengthens at every advance, and at last takes
> possession of the whole soul so absolutely, that a man sees
> nothing in the world of importance to others or himself, but
> in his object.

Avarice, Adams suggested, could not be brought under the control of calculative reason. The "love of gold" and the other aristocratic passions tended to subdue not just the weaker passions
but "even the understanding itself, if not the conscience too,

until they become absolute and imperious masters of the whole mind."[41]

Just as the desire for wealth and the aversion to poverty could not be accounted for in terms of economic rationality, neither could such passions be explained by the ethical superiority thought to accompany riches. "Ask your reason," wrote Adams, "what disgrace there can be in poverty?" Had moral philosophy provided any good reason to prefer wealth to indigence?

> What moral sentiment of approbation, praise, or honor can there be in a palace? What dishonor in a cottage? What glory in a coach? What shame in a wagon? Is not the sense of propriety and sense of merit as much connected with an empty purse as a full one? May not a man be as estimable, amiable, and respectable, attended by his faithful dog, as if preceded and followed by a train of horses and servants?

However moral philosophers might respond, Adams was sure that observation of human behavior revealed the simple answer that "the gaudy trappings of wealth" enjoy in the eyes of mankind an immense respectability—more, even, than "genius or learning, wisdom or virtue."[42]

Sympathy and Power

How would the newly invigorated passion for wealth effect the distribution of power? Alexis de Tocqueville would later emphasize the leveling aspects of the universal love of wealth. "The first thing that strikes one in the United States," he would note, "is the innumerable multitude of those who seek to get out of their original condition." An American could not be found who was not "devoured by the desire to rise."[43] Tocqueville believed that America ran the long-term risk of recreating an aristocracy. The exploding demand for manufactured goods threatened to draw men of great wealth and enlightenment to the management of industry, and the routinized division of labor rendered workers less industrious and more dependent on their industrial masters.[44] But according to Tocqueville, the pervasive love of money in the United States was, by and large, a leveling force. The ambition for riches, having displaced old notions of aristocratic greatness and put the ambitions of all Americans on the same plane, had a profound equalizing effect on the national character. Ambition was no longer the preserve of an aristocratic class but was instead "the universal sentiment" in America.[45]

For Adams, in contrast, the universal regard paid to wealth all but guaranteed that the wealthy would hold disproportionate political power. It was true that the widespread passion for wealth had something of an egalitarian aspect. Emulation and the scramble for riches, said Adams, "takes place in every neighborhood, in every family; among artisans, husbandmen, laborers, as much as between dukes and marquises."[46] But it was also true that because most people sought distinction through the acquisition of riches, wealth would become the predominant marker of social distinction and, therefore, the chief object of public sympathy. Echoing Adam Smith, Adams observed that sympathy for the rich was as pronounced in the modern commercial republic as it had ever been. In modern London, as much as in ancient Rome, the public would more readily sympathize with the righteously condemned rich man than with the plight of the poor man of virtue who suffered from "the unjust violence of men." Moreover, Adams believed that public sympathy for wealth generated oligarchic influence because the sympathetic public would be inclined to *follow* the rich. In *Discourses on Davila*, he quoted Smith's description of the "disposition of mankind . . . to go along with all the passions of the rich and the powerful." Following Smith's logic, he believed that our own passion for wealth as a sign of distinction and happiness leads us to cheer for the rich. We become "eager to assist them" in attaining what in our view is "a system of happiness that approaches so near to perfection."[47]

We see then that Adams understood wealth to be powerful on account of its status as a glaring marker of social distinction and therefore as an attractive object of sympathy. It is worth pausing to note that Adams's view of social distinction as a source of power explains an oddity of his political thought: his repeated references to beauty as a source of aristocratic power. As we have seen, Adams frequently paired wealth and birth together as powerful, though unmeritocratic, sources of aristocracy. He contrasted wealth and birth (the goods of fortune) with meritocratic qualities like wisdom and virtue (the goods of the mind). In *Discourses on Davila*, Adams oddly included a discussion of beauty alongside remarks on wealth and birth, as if to include it among those goods of fortune that reliably translate into aristocratic power. He later defended this categorization in a retirement-era letter to Jefferson in which he insisted that beauty, like wealth and birth, would tend to overpower those qualities associated with merit. "What chance have talents and virtues, in competition with wealth and birth . . . and beauty?" Not much of one. "The five pillars of aristocracy are beauty, wealth, birth, genius, and virtue," he wrote. "Any one of the three first can, at any time, overbear any one or both of the two last." The aristocratic power of beauty, like that of wealth and birth, would persist despite advances in education. "Now, my friend," he asked Jefferson, "who are the [*aristoi*]?" Adams anticipated Jefferson's answer and offered his own: "Philosophers may answer, 'the wise and good.' But the world, mankind, have, by their practice, always answered, 'the rich, the beautiful, and well-born.'" Indeed, Adams went as far as to say that beauty and its related qualities have often prevailed not just over merit but over *all* competing qualities. "Beauty, grace, figure, attitude, movement, have, in innumerable instances, prevailed over wealth, birth, talents, virtues, and every thing else."[48]

In a letter to John Taylor of Caroline, Adams described beauty as a potent source of aristocratic power. "Socrates calls beauty a short-lived tyranny; Plato, *the privilege of nature*; Theophrastus, a mute eloquence; Diogenes, the best letter of recommendation; Carneades, a queen without soldiers; Theocritus, a serpent covered with flowers." But the influence of beauty was not a mere relic of ancient aristocracies. It continued to have "as much influence in one form of government as in any other," producing an aristocratic class "in the deepest democracy that ever was known or imagined, as infallibly as in any other form of government." If one denied the natural influence of the beautiful, Adams wrote, he should read the history of beauty from Eve to Madame Du Barry. And it was not only beautiful women themselves who wielded influence on account of their beauty but also, and perhaps especially, their male relations: "Can you believe, Mr. Taylor, that the brother of such a sister, the father of such a daughter, the husband of such a wife, or even the gallant of such a mistress, would have but one vote in your moral republic?" For both its possessor and her relations, beauty was a source of influence, "according to Plato and to truth."[49]

"You may laugh," Adams wrote Jefferson, "at the introduction of beauty among the pillars of aristocracy." Indeed, all this talk of an aristocracy of beauty probably perplexed Adams's readers. But Adams's insistence on the power of beauty makes sense once considered in the context of his social-psychological theory of power. As outlined above, Adam Smith and other eighteenth-century writers thought that power belongs not just to those capable of physical or material domination but also to those most socially distinguished. Beauty was, according to Adams, among the chief guarantors of social distinction. This effect could be seen by the enormous value that so many attributed to beauty in spite of the fact that the possession of beauty yielded very little benefit in terms of pleasure. The pleasure received at the sight of beautiful things is at best "but a slight sensation, and of shortest continuance." And even the pleasure of a beautiful husband or wife is fleeting, as "a very short familiarity totally destroys all sense and attention to such properties." Meanwhile, "a very little time and habit destroy all the aversion to ugliness and deformity, when unattended with disease or ill temper." The true rationale for seeking beauty was not for pleasure but for the consideration and power that would accompany it. For just as wealth was empowered by the admiration and sympathy it attracted, beauty tended to "command the notice and attention of the public" and was often "courted and admired . . . more than discretion, wit, sense, and many other accomplishments and virtues, of infinitely more importance to the happiness of private life, as well as to the utility and ornament of society."[50]

The fact that Adams consistently mentioned beauty alongside wealth as a chief source of oligarchic power highlights the extent to which his explanation of oligarchy was not strictly material but also aesthetic. Adams was at pains to point out that wealth, like beauty, owed its power in large part to its glittering distinction. It was true, as Adams wrote in his *Defence*, that much of the power of wealth derived from various social connections and material dependencies. But as with the radiance of beauty, the glare of wealth had a powerful independent effect. For even "among the wisest people that live," Adams insisted, "there is a degree of admiration, abstracted from all dependence, obligation, expectation, or even acquaintance, which accompanies splendid wealth, insures some respect, and bestows some influence."[51]

It is a trope of contemporary American politics that ordinary Americans often share the political preferences of the rich—such as opposition to progressive taxation—because those citizens hope themselves one day to become rich. As the social commentator David Brooks has put it, Americans vote their aspirations, not their immediate self-interests: "They have always had a sense that great opportunities lie just over the horizon, in the next valley, with the next job or the next big thing. None of us is really poor; we're just pre-rich."[52] But this is not quite the sentiment that Adams described. According to Adams's theory, there is no calculation of long-term gain involved in our sympathy for the rich. As Adam Smith observed, "We desire to serve them for their own sake, without any other recompense but the vanity or the honor of obliging them."[53] Sympathy is a vicarious passion. When we sympathize with the rich and follow them in their pursuits, we merely indulge the vanity of celebrating their out-of-reach success. We expect nothing tangible in return. To put it another way, when we vote with the rich we do not vote our interests or aspirations, only our egos.

On this account, it was not chiefly the hopes and dreams of the poor that empowered the wealthy. Nor were the rich powerful merely on account of their material capacity to subdue ordinary citizens. The rich were empowered on account of their tendency to stand out, to be recognized, and to evoke favorable public sentiments. Again, the contrast with the influential account of Alexis de Tocqueville is instructive. Tocqueville found the rich to be politically frustrated in America. The proud equality of Americans humbled the wealthy and demanded that they abandon pretensions to superiority. The richest citizens, unable to "sustain an often unequal struggle against the poorest of their fellow citizens," preferred instead to withdraw from political life. "Not being able to take up a rank in public life analogous to the one they occupy in private life, they abandon the first to concentrate on the second."[54] Even as the rich man publicly extols the advantages of democratic forms, he in fact "submits to this state of things as to an irremediable evil." In many respects, Adams's thought on the place of wealth in American democracy was the mirror image of Tocqueville's later analysis.[55] Where Tocqueville would emphasize the discontinuity between European aristocracy and the American rich, Adams observed European hierarchies and emphasized the extent to which American society would reproduce them. There was no reason, he insisted, to think that wealth in America would not enjoy the sympathy it had affected in Europe. "Riches Grandeur and Power," Adams wrote to Jefferson in 1787, "will have the same effect upon American as it has upon European minds."[56] "I assure you, my friend," he wrote to Benjamin Rush in 1789, "I wish my dear Countrymen had less Vanity and more Pride." But the manners in Boston, in New York, and in Philadelphia were not essentially different from those in the cities of Europe. "The advantages we have over Europe are chiefly geographical," Adams lamented. "I see very little moral or political Preference. As far as I can judge there is as much vice, Folly, and more Infidelity, Idleness, Luxury and Dissipation, in any of our great Towns in Proportion to Numbers, as in London."[57]

If the rich could not be expected to withdraw from public affairs, it was also inconceivable that a public-spirited elite of the kind Jefferson had imagined could be elevated to power. As Adams had insisted again and again in his retirement-era writings, the ambitions of elites would follow the sentiments of the public. In his commentary on the Abbé de Mably's *De le legislation*, Adams suggested that magistrates in corrupt regimes sought pomp and luxury not just as ends in themselves but also because these things appealed to the people. Similarly, in his commentary on Mary Wollstonecraft's *Historical and Moral View of the Origin and Progress of the French Revolution,* he rejected Wollstonecraft's notion that the morals of the French people had been corrupted by despotic rulers. The truth, wrote Adams, was that wealth and commerce affected rulers and ruled alike and that it was just as likely for corruption to proceed from the governed to the governors. In a society corrupted by wealth and commerce, it was folly to expect the ambitious to emulate the most virtuous. The only emulation in such an environment would be in "profligacy, hypocrisy and villainy." "Emulation in virtue can only be where virtue is respected."[58]

The Pride of Wealth

If sympathy for the rich tended to generate oligarchic power, Adams believed that this tendency would only be exacerbated by the conditions that prevailed in post-Revolution America. In the *Defence*, Adams had described the love of money and the pursuit of luxury as pervasive in American society. Following the Revolution, "the Americans found an unusual quantity of money flow in upon them, and, without the least degree of prudence, foresight, consideration, or measure, rushed headlong into a greater degree of luxury than ought to have crept in for a hundred years." The frantic pursuit of luxury was closely related to the equality of free peoples: "A free people are the most addicted to luxury of any. That equality which they enjoy, and in which they glory, inspires them with sentiments which hurry them to luxury."[59] Alexis de Tocqueville would similarly describe the extent to which wealth had become, in democratic America, the preeminent mark of distinction. Indeed, the democratization of society went hand in hand with a pervasive desire for riches. In America there was very little of the old aristocratic ambition—the noble desire to be publically recognized for great deeds, yet ambition had not disappeared in America, it had only taken new form. The love of wealth, a passion that peoples of earlier times had considered a form of cupidity, had been elevated by Americans to the status of a "noble and estimable ambition." Given that only a violent pursuit of material well-being could effectively exploit America's vast resources, Americans praised the scramble for wealth and even made "a sort of virtue of commercial recklessness."[60]

Prior to the wave of democratic revolution that swept across the Atlantic world, there had existed forms of distinction that competed with wealth for preeminence. Aristocratic republics had understood the corrupting influence of wealth and so had balanced the "pride of birth" against the "pride of wealth."[61] But this counterweight had been removed with the abolition of nobility. Much like Edmund Burke, who worried that the Revolution would elevate commercial life to such a degree as to "make speculation as extensive as life," Adams worried that the Revolution would have the unintended consequence of focusing all energies on the pursuit of gain.[62]

Adams was far from believing that hereditary nobility should be reintroduced in America. Whatever counter-oligarchic role such families had played in the past, nobility was neither desirable nor possible in an American nation that allowed none to rise above the social station of "the people." Adams insisted, however, that in the absence of aristocratic families, republican America would, through its sympathies, elevate its own elite— an elite that would lack the pomp and ceremony of formal nobility but not its power.

If John Adams feared oligarchy more than many future analysts of American politics, this was in part because he perceived a subtle, almost intangible, mechanism by which wealth might translate into political power. It is a widely shared intuition among those concerned about the political power of wealth in our time that money commands influence by purchasing it. Money, wrote Samuel Huntington, "becomes evil not when it is used to buy goods but when it is used to buy power."[63] If modern democracies face the imminent danger of corruption by wealth, it is predicted that such corruption will be the result of lavish campaign contributions, near-limitless lobbying expenditures, and the appropriation of media space by the superrich. Just as the economic power of money derives from its ability to purchase goods and services, the *political* power of money is thought to derive from its ability to buy votes, politicians, and policies. John Adams, a keen observer of the emerging commercial republic and a close reader of the moral psychology of the eighteenth-century Scottish Enlightenment, raised the possibility that wealth wields influence for a different reason—not merely on account of its purchasing power, but also on account of its capacity to attract the sympathy of the public.

If the notion of power derived from sympathy and admiration is foreign to today's students of wealth and politics, it is not unknown to scholars of international relations. As Joseph Nye has argued, physical coercion and economic incentives— "carrots" and "sticks"—are not the only available forms of power. There is also "soft" power, the ability to get what one wants through *attraction*. In the case of American foreign policy, soft power is generated by favorable sentiments felt for the United States by the world's people. Attraction to America's culture and political ideals leads others, through admiration, to want what the United States wants and to follow it willingly.[64] It was a soft form of power that John Adams and his Scottish antecedents believed belonged to the wealthy in commercial republics. The power of riches was not only the ability to coerce through relations of material dependency or to induce through direct payments but also the power to seduce through admiration and sympathy. The source of oligarchic power lay not merely in material necessity and self-interest, but in the less tangible but no less potent realm of the moral sentiments.

If oligarchic power originated, in part, in widespread public sentiments, what could be done to contain it? As we will see in chapter 4, the answer suggested in Adams's political writings involved an area of institutional design that modern political science has largely neglected: dignified titles.

CHAPTER FOUR

Dignified Democracy

The object of public admiration will invariably be
the object of the wishes of individuals, and if
one has to be rich in order to shine then being
rich will always be the dominant passion.

—JEAN-JACQUES ROUSSEAU,
Considerations on the Government in Poland

Titles never die in America, although we *do* take a
republican pride in poking fun at such trifles.

—MARK TWAIN AND CHARLES DUDLEY WARNER,
The Gilded Age

THERE IS ONE EPISODE of John Adams's career that has
long been singled out as an object of derision: his defense of honorific titles. To the surprise of his contemporaries,
Adams began his tenure as the nation's first vice president with
a campaign to persuade Congress to attach dignified titles and
ceremonial displays to the institutions of the new republic. Insisting that the American people desired a government that
was "dignified and respectable," he sought for the Senate's reply
to the president's first inaugural address to include a reference
to the "dignity and splendor" of the new government. Most
notoriously, he sought to attach to the president the title "His

Highness the President of the United States of America and Protector of the Rights of the Same."[1]

Adams was mercilessly mocked and ridiculed for his position. How could this esteemed republican leader, chosen for leadership largely on the strength of his revolutionary credentials, so readily embrace antirepublican titles once in office? To his contemporaries this appeared to be a complete about-face and, worse yet, an apostasy. By defending what looked like monarchic and aristocratic institutions, Adams was lending credence to the worst fear of those who had opposed the new national system: that the new Constitution would place America on an inexorable path toward monarchic and aristocratic rule.

The perception that Adams harbored a love of titles was deeply damaging to his reputation in the early years of his vice presidency. And though he would retain sufficient credibility to be elected as the nation's second president, his apparent elitism set him starkly at odds with a growing tide of democratic sentiment, a tide that would eventually sweep him from office and replace him with Thomas Jefferson, who would deliberately fashion himself as a plain public servant and a man of the people with no taste for frivolous dignities.

To Adams's bitter frustration, his contemporaries never made a genuine effort to understand his true views regarding honorific titles. Just as critics had misconstrued his *Defence of the Constitutions* as an apology for aristocracy, they likewise twisted his defense of titles into a position that was irredeemably antirepublican. The truth was that Adams viewed titles as not just compatible with the republican form of government but also as necessary for its success. An honorific "language of signs"[2] would be necessary, he argued, to motivate the kind of publicly beneficial behavior that republics require. And moreover, Adams's critics overlooked his argument that, in modern commercial republics, titles would also perform a counter-oligarchic function.

In societies in which admiration and sympathy would naturally accrue to the rich, honorary titles could check this oligarchic tendency by competing with wealth for the favorable sentiments of the public.

"His Rotundity"

The most complete account of the Senate's debate over honorific titles was recorded in the journal of William Maclay, a backcountry Pennsylvania senator who led the opposition to Adams's effort. Maclay found all such dignities to be contrary to the sentiments of the people. To Adams's insistence that government be made "dignified and respectable," Maclay objected that such dignities were precisely what opponents of the Federal Constitution anticipated when they predicted there would be a "transition from it to kingly government and all the trappings and splendor of royalty." There was no doubt in Maclay's mind that the American people would perceive the establishment of these formalities as "the first step of the ladder in the ascent to royalty." The word "splendor," after all, called to mind "all the faulty finery, brilliant scenes, and expensive trappings of royal government"—a vision, in other words that was "quite the reverse of republican respectability," which Maclay associated with "firm and prudent councils, frugality, and economy."[3]

On this account, Adams's sensitivity on the issue of titles could be viewed as pathetic and even laughable. Maclay described the vice president's anxiety during the debate. Which precedent, Adams desperately asked, did the framers have in mind when designing executive offices? Did they envision "the two kings of Sparta, the two consuls of Rome, or the two suffetes of Carthage?" And what about the furniture? Did the architect of the Senate consult the Constitution when including a wide chair, *with room for two*, in the chamber? Most of all, Adams fretted about the dignity (or lack of it) attached to his own office: "Gentlemen, I feel great difficulty how to act. I am possessed of two separate powers. . . . I am Vice-President. In this I am nothing, but I may be everything. But I am president also of the Senate. When the President comes into the Senate, what shall I be?" The vice president's distress was so palpable as to be embarrassing for all involved. Maclay recorded that Adams, "as if oppressed with a sense of his distressed situation . . . threw himself back in his chair." Maclay could not help but smirk when the vice president's frantic questions were met with awkward silence. "God forgive me, for it was involuntary, but the profane muscles of my face were in tune for laughter in spite of my indisposition."[4]

Yet Maclay insisted that the episode was no laughing matter, for it revealed the intention of Adams and his followers to establish hereditary ranks of royalty and nobility in America. Unlike many revolutionaries, for whom the "abolishing of royalty, the extinguishment of patronage and dependencies attached to that form of government, were the exalted motives," Adams belonged to a separate camp that "cared for nothing else but a translation of the diadem and scepter from London to Boston, New York, or Philadelphia." The spirit of such men was the same that had manifested itself in the Society of the Cincinnati, a hereditary membership society formed by former officers of the Continental Army. Adams and his kind sought nothing less than "the creation of a new monarchy in America, and to form niches for themselves in the temple of royalty." How odd it was, wrote Maclay, that Americans were manifesting such a spirit of royalism at the very moment when a spirit of freedom was breaking out in France. "Strange, indeed, that in that very country . . . where the flame of freedom had been kindled, an attempt should be made to introduce these absurdities and humiliating distinctions which the hand of reason, aided by our example, was prostrating in the heart of Europe."[5]

Adams was of course defeated in his efforts and embarrassed in the process. In exchange for his stubborn effort to attach honor to the presidency, he was rewarded only with derision. The Senate eventually resolved to address the chief executive simply as "President of the United States." One senator did, however, grant the portly and diminutive vice president a new title of his own: "His Rotundity."[6]

The problems for his reputation were only exacerbated when, with characteristic stubbornness, Adams took the fight to the press. In the essays that composed his *Discourses on Davila*, which appeared in the *Gazette of the United States* in 1790, he wrote explicitly about the need for titles. "The wisdom and virtue of all nations," he lectured, "have endeavored to regulate the passion for respect and distinction, and to reduce it to some order in society, by titles marking the gradations of magistracy." Predictably, this message was widely ridiculed by critics who belonged to an emerging coalition of politicians and locally organized political clubs who understood themselves to be genuine "republicans" seeking to uphold the principles of the revolution in the face of a cast of "monarchists" and "Tories."[7]

Among those who viewed Adams's defense of titles with suspicion was Secretary of State Thomas Jefferson, and the controversy surrounding Adams's apparent royalism was heightened when Jefferson accidentally made his suspicions publicly known. In the process of arranging for the publication of an American edition of Thomas Paine's *Rights of Man*, a work in which Paine defended the French Revolution and linked its ideals to those of the United States, Jefferson sent a copy of the work to a publisher with a note attached that was intended only for the editor's private notice. The note, which to Jefferson's embarrassment later appeared as a preface to the published American edition, described Paine's work as an antidote to an emerging antirepublican ideology. When Jefferson remarked in the note that he was pleased "that something is at length to be publickly said against the political heresies which have sprung up among us," his readers were well aware that the "heresies" mentioned were those of Vice President Adams.[8]

From the perspective of his critics, Adams's seeming fascination with frivolous dignities proved that he was hopelessly out of touch with the democratic tide of the new nation. This perception was strengthened by the emerging division between Federalists and their "Democratic-Republican" rivals. Adams and Jefferson, the respective standard-bearers of the two parties, likewise became associated with two different postures regarding honorific titles. The contrast was never more apparent than during Jefferson's first inaugural ceremony. Four years earlier, Adams had arrived at his inaugural in an elegant new carriage with liveries for his coachman and footman, and he himself had worn a resplendent new suit with a cockaded hat under his arm. In contrast, Jefferson chose to arrive at his inaugural on foot. As one reporter observed, the third president was dressed as "a plain citizen, without any distinctive badge of office." Unlike both Adams and Washington before him, he did not carry a ceremonial sword.[9]

It was odd that Jefferson became the symbol of republican simplicity while Adams came to be caricatured as a would-be monarchist obsessed with frivolous honors and dignities. It was Adams, after all, who described himself as a "plebeian" even while serving in high office,[10] whereas Jefferson, as we have discussed, self-identified as a "natural aristocrat."[11] The truth was that Adams never loved titles for their own sake. He agreed with his critics that titles were essentially frivolous. "In my private character," he wrote to Benjamin Rush, "I despise [titles]

as much at least as any Quaker or philosopher on earth." Insofar as such distinctions were important, they were important
in spite of their frivolity. As we will see, Adams believed they
were important not for their intrinsic value but for their capacity
to govern passions. Such "marks and signs," he wrote, "attract
the attention of mankind more than parts or learning, virtue or
religion." The fact that titles are not endowed with any intrinsic
moral importance did not make them unimportant for political
science. In the *Discourses* Adams conveyed this point by drawing on Shakespeare's plays *The Tempest* and *Macbeth* to evoke
the thought of a dying man pondering the pettiness of worldly
titles:

> A death bed, it is said, shows the emptiness of titles. That may
> be. But does it not equally show the futility of riches, power,
> liberty, and all earthly things? "The cloud-capt towers, the
> gorgeous palaces, the solemn temples, the great globe itself,"
> appear "the baseless fabric of a vision," and "life itself, a tale,
> told by an idiot, full of sound and fury, signifying nothing."
> Shall it be inferred from this, that fame, liberty, property, and
> life, shall be always despised and neglected? Shall laws and
> government, which regulate sublunary things, be neglected
> because they appear baubles at the hour of death?

Adams conceded to his critics that titles were essentially
"empty," and from a moral-philosophical perspective they were
perhaps even embarrassing. But owing to the power they exercised on the psyche, titles were no less important for political
science, for none could deny that even in austere republics, titles
were "sought with ardor, very often, by men possessed in the
most eminent degree, of all the more solid advantages of birth
and fortune, merit and services, with the best faculties of the
head, and the most engaging recommendations of the heart."[12]

Adams never shared the assumption that honorific titles were inextricably bound up with monarchy or aristocracy. In a letter to Jefferson that he wrote upon discovering Jefferson's accusatory statement in his preface to Paine's *Rights of Man*, he denied all charges of antirepublicanism:

> If You suppose that I have or ever had a design or desire, of attempting to introduce a Government of King, Lords and Commons, or in other Words an hereditary Executive, or an hereditary Senate . . . you are wholly mistaken. There is not such a Thought expressed or intimated in any public writing or private Letter of mine, and I may safely challenge all Mankind to produce such a passage and quote the Chapter and Verse.[13]

As we will see, Adams believed that honorific titles were perfectly compatible with the emerging democratic-republican order. And though not valuable for their own sake, titles could nonetheless be defended for principled reasons. As we will see, Adams understood titles as instruments for spurring ambitious individuals to exert themselves in service of the public good. And most important for our discussion, he also believed that titles could serve to counteract the oligarchic tendencies of modern republics.

THE LANGUAGE OF SIGNS

Despite all of the suspicions of his critics, there was never compelling evidence that Adams yearned for nobility. He agreed that titles of nobility were unacceptable in a republic, but he insisted that republican principles were entirely compatible with titles of *office*. In a retirement-era letter to Mercy Otis Warren, his close friend who had recently published the three-volume

History of the American Revolution, Adams reprimanded her for the "insinuations about Titles and titled nobility" that she had included in her history, insinuations that he supposed "were intended as Sarcasms upon me." He insisted that what Warren missed was that "Titles of office are very different from Titles of Nobility." Titles of office were not hereditary and nor were they guaranteed for life. Indeed, one could point to many such titles of office, in America and elsewhere, that had nothing to do with nobility:

> The Title of your Worship or your Honour, or your Excellency is no Mark of an hereditary Nobility in any Country, certainly not in this, any more than the Title of Colonel or Major General. The Title of Excellency is given in Europe to Ambassadors, Commanders in Chief of Armies or Fleets, to Governors of Provinces . . . but none of these are hereditary.

Moreover, if democratic-republican ideology denounced titles, the citizenry had not stopped desiring them: "There is not a Country under Heaven in which Titles and Precedency are more eagerly coveted than in this Country." Rattling off a long list of American titles from "Major-General" to the simple title of "Drummer," Adams insisted that titles continued to be pursued in America "with as furious Zeal as that of Earl Marquis or Duke in any other Country."[14]

And yet, if Adams believed in titles of office and not titles of nobility, it was true nonetheless that he viewed titles as necessary for maintaining a certain degree of social and political subordination. As we have seen, alongside Adams's lifelong preoccupation with the danger posed by social and economic elites was a fear of disorder and lawlessness.[15] When arguing for the necessity of titles, Adams repeatedly invoked the danger to stable authority posed by lack of respect for high offices. To clarify his point in a letter to his friend Benjamin Rush, he suggested that he might one day write a play entitled "Government without Title." The play would present a Quaker and his wife along with ten children and four servants, all of whom would "live without form." All would live together in the same room, eat together at the same table, and "promiscuously call each other by their names without Titles." The result, Adams writes, would be chaotic insubordination, with sons marrying female servants and daughters marrying male servants. The end result would be anarchy, because both children and servants "would soon kick and cuff the old man and woman."[16]

This kind of argument suggests that the worries of Adams's critics were not entirely groundless. Though he did not accept a strict rank ordering of society, he did wish to maintain certain relations of deference between citizens and high officials. While in Europe, he had witnessed firsthand the manner in which such relations were supported by titles. There is nothing, he wrote, that "strikes and overawes the most abandoned of the Populace so much as Titles."[17] Even if such a statement was not clear evidence of sympathy for monarchy or aristocracy, it did seem to reveal a certain sympathy for social deference that was contrary to the revolutionary spirit.

Yet if Adams believed that titles would maintain deferential social relations, he also believed that titles would perform important republican, and even counter-oligarchic, functions. For one thing, he thought that titles could channel the energies of the most ambitious away from destructive self-interest and toward public-spirited activity. And more important for our discussion, he also thought that titles could counteract the oligarchic passions that tended to characterize commercial republics. As we have seen, Adams believed that wealth gained power in commercial societies through the inclination of the citizenry to admire wealth and to sympathize with the rich. Honorary titles, Adams suggested, could mitigate this tendency by competing with wealth for the admiration and sympathy of the public.

Adams took after the many historical writers who had discussed the role of honor in politics. In much the same way that economic writers of the modern era would argue that the self-interested behavior of the marketplace could contribute to the public interest, observers of the Roman republic found that self-regarding desires for honor could motivate publicly beneficial activity. The historian Sallust influentially described the manner in which Roman citizens esteemed valor above riches and were pitted against one another in competition for public glory. In Rome, wrote Sallust, "each man strove to be first to strike down the foe, to scale a wall to be seen by all while doing such a deed."[18] Once the kingship had been abolished and merit was no longer held in suspicion, men's minds were filled with a "thirst for glory" that made Rome strong and great in a short period of time. As Augustine wrote centuries later, the Romans' desire for glory enabled them to restrain their baser desires. According to him, the greatness of the Romans fell far short of that virtue, which issues from devout faith and the love of beauty. But nonetheless, the Romans' "love of praise" had spurred them to accomplish "marvelous achievements, which were, no doubt, praiseworthy and glorious in men's estimation."[19]

More recently, Montesquieu had described the role of honor in well-ordered monarchies. Republics, small in scale, relied on public-spirited citizens to look after the public good. Large-scale monarchies, whose subjects lacked the kind of self-denying virtue that is possible in republics, relied instead upon "honor," which Montesquieu understood in psychological terms as a desire for distinction and praise. The honor motive served the public good in spite of its self-regarding nature, and it did so primarily on account of its effect on the arrangement of political power. In a well-ordered monarchy, military men, lawyers, and other ambitious individuals designated as "nobility" were spurred by the honor motive to defend their constitutional rights against the incursions of the crown. The nobility thereby became an intermediary body protecting the liberty of subjects from the otherwise unlimited power of the monarch.[20]

Many Founding Era Americans believed that this type of desire for distinction could be of great use in the new republic.[21] Montesquieu had thought that monarchies, not republics, were uniquely capable of benefitting from the honor motive owing to the fact that "it is the nature of honour to aspire to preferments and titles" and that it was in monarchies that such ranks and titles abounded. But for such figures as Hamilton, Madison, and Adams, the republican character of America's constitution did not preclude the need to harness the desire for distinction. In the *Federalist*, Hamilton referred to "the love of fame" as "the ruling passion of the noblest minds," and he insisted that government be so designed as to harness that passion to spur men to "undertake extensive and arduous enterprises for the public benefit."[22] Likewise, Madison insisted that those designing governmental institutions must not assume a disinterested humanity. Indeed, the entire machinery of the new federal government— checks and balances, recurring elections, and the separation of powers—was built on the assumption that government officials and citizens alike would often seek, out of personal ambition, to encroach upon the rights and prerogatives of others. "If men were angels," Madison wrote in the *Federalist*, "no government would be necessary. If angels were to govern men, neither external nor internal controls on government would be necessary." But in the absence of angels, "ambition must be made to counteract ambition." When designing a government "administered by men over men," it was imperative not only to assume self-regarding passions but also to harness them as "a sentinel over the public rights."[23]

No Founding Era thinker wrote more about the need to harness self-regarding passions than did John Adams. Though it is true that in his early writings Adams portrayed republican politics as dependent on disinterested virtue, in his mature writings he changed course. Virtue, whether in its Christian, moral, or political variety, "cannot be too much beloved, practised, or rewarded," he wrote in the *Defence*. But it was a grave mistake to follow Montesquieu and seek to make virtue the foundation of a republican order. After all, the features of Montesquieu's virtuous republic had never characterized any nation. No republic in history was entirely free of avarice and ambition, and neither was it true that "any people ever existed who loved the public better than themselves, their private friends, neighbors, &c." The virtue of frugality that Montesquieu attributed to republics, moreover, had never been practiced by choice, only by the necessity of poverty. "Poor nations only are frugal," he wrote, "rich ones always profuse." Finally, the love of equality that Montesquieu had attributed to democratic republics had existed only in a very limited sense: "Every man hates to have a superior, but no man is willing to have an equal; every man desires to be superior to all others."[24] In other words, the democratic man did not despise inequality so much as inferiority. All of these considerations taken together meant that modern commercial republics, pervaded as they were by self-regarding desires for distinction, could not expect to substitute disinterestedness for avarice and self-serving ambition.

As we have seen, Adams believed that in America and elsewhere men were motivated chiefly by what he called the "passion for distinction," a desire to be recognized, esteemed, and praised by others. It was a passion that yearned for titles and signs of dignity. Similar to Montesquieu's description of monarchies as channeling the desire for prominence by the use of titles and preferments, Adams insisted that republics needed titles to govern the passion for distinction. He observed that in the republics of Europe there was "a more constant and anxious attention" to titles than there was in the monarchies. Even in small villages, "little employments and trifling distinctions are contended for with equal eagerness, as honors and offices in commonwealths and kingdoms."[25]

Thus, rather than turning to monarchies for examples of the proper employment of titles, Adams found his exemplary model in the Roman republic. The Romans understood that if a republic were to motivate its citizens to serve the public good, it was not enough to appeal to the disinterested reason of the citizenry. Reason could serve as a guide that points one in the direction of virtuous action, but only the passions could reliably spur one to act. "Reason holds the helm, but passions are the gales." It was not enough, then, to use rational exhortation to motivate action for the common good. Instead, it was necessary to employ a "language of signs"—a language that appealed not to reason but to the senses. In order to motivate men to strive for meritorious achievements and to pursue important public offices, it was necessary to adorn offices and accomplishments with alluring displays. This was why in Rome, "every thing in religion, government, and common life, among the Romans, was parade, representation, and ceremony." It was why consuls, senators, and tribunes wore large, flowing robes fashioned in varying colors and sizes to reflect different ranks and stations. Ivory chairs, lictors, rods, crowns, and ceremonial ovations all operated to channel the emulation of the citizens and to harness self-regarding passions for the good of the public.[26]

As we will see, Adams thought that the language of signs could also serve another purpose. Apart from the role of harnessing ambition for the public good, signs could also excite the

admiration and sympathy of the public. In a commercial republic that would tend toward widespread sympathy for the rich,
dignified public offices could stand as rival objects of public sentiment and thereby check the oligarchic influence of wealth.

DEMOCRACY AND DIGNITY

As we have seen in previous chapters, Adams believed that the
goods of fortune—birth, beauty, and especially wealth—would
retain a great deal of power in modern republics in spite of the
advent of free and equal citizenship. Fortune had always enjoyed natural advantages, and that situation was only exacerbated in the modern commercial republic, where democratic leveling had unintentionally made wealth the preeminent marker
of distinction and the most exalted object of emulation. In the
old regime, there existed markers of distinction that could compete with personal fortune for preeminence. Before the era of
revolution, Adams pointed out, nations had used pride of family
as a check on pride of wealth. Those states had understood that
the immense consideration paid to wealth, the "sordid scramble for money," tended to generate social vices such as "treach-
ery, cowardice, and a selfish, unsocial meanness" and that the
prejudice in favor of noble families generated a certain pride
in talents and virtues and also "the maxims and principles of
religion, morals, and government." Observing this, nations had
employed the prejudice of birth to counteract the prejudice of
wealth. Modern republics, meanwhile, were abandoning that
counterweight. Invoking the national assembly of France, Adams asked whether the new republic could withstand the avaricious passions unleashed by the abolition of nobility: "What
effect on the moral character of the nation would be produced,
by destroying, if that were possible, all attention to families, and

setting all the passions on the pursuit of gain?" Was it not inevitable, Adams asked, that the passions of avarice left unchecked would result in "universal venality and an incorrigible corruption in elections"?[27]

On this point Adams concurred with Edmund Burke, who in his *Reflections on the Revolution in France* argued that those "unhappy corruptions" that had previously afflicted only the wealthy had been diffused by the revolution through all the ranks of society. Burke vividly described the avaricious passions set in motion by the French Revolution:

> Your legislators, in everything new, are the very first who have founded a commonwealth upon gaming, and infused this spirit into it as its vital breath. The great object in these politics is to metamorphose France from a great kingdom into one great playtable; to turn its inhabitants into a nation of gamesters; to make speculation as extensive as life; to mix it with all its concerns and to divert the whole of the hopes and fears of the people from their usual channels into the impulses, passions, and superstitions of those who live on chances.[28]

Adams did not follow the likes of Burke in defending traditional aristocracy as a bulwark against crass commercialism. The American people would reject the form of aristocratic snobbery that sought to defend hereditary honor from bourgeois corruption.[29] "In America," Adams wrote in the *Defence*, "the vainest of all must be of the people, or be nothing." Recognition of noble families would "justly excite universal indignation." In a system in which "every office is equally open to every competitor, and the people must decide upon every pretension to a place in the legislature, that of governor and senator, as well as representative," wrote Adams, "no such airs will ever be endured." Nonetheless, he found such institutions to have served an important counter-oligarchic function:

> That kind of pride, which looks down on commerce and manufactures as degrading, may, indeed, in many countries of Europe, be a useful and necessary quality in the nobility. It may prevent, in some degree, the whole nation from being entirely delivered up to the spirit of avarice. It may be the cause why honor is preferred by some to money. It may prevent the nobility from becoming too rich, and acquiring too large a proportion of the landed property.

It was true that in America orders of nobility "would not only be mischievous, but would expose the highest pretensions of the kind to universal ridicule and contempt."[30] But for Adams it was important to admit that, in the absence of formal aristocracy, modern democracy would empower its own elite. If American principles rejected nobility, American sympathies would fill the void by elevating the status of wealth.

Adams never yearned for titles of nobility, but he did hope that titles of office might function as hereditary titles had once done: to counteract oligarchic passions. Oddly enough, Adams may have found a precedent for this idea in the writings of an Enlightenment thinker whose name has long been closely associated with modern ideals of democracy and popular sovereignty: Jean-Jacques Rousseau.[31] In *Considerations on the Government in Poland*, in which he recommended reforms to the Polish-Lithuanian commonwealth, Rousseau emphasized the role of illustrious offices and signs of rank in counteracting popular passions for material wealth. For Rousseau, the passion for luxury among the citizens resulted in large part from the exalted status of wealth and the widespread admiration of the rich: "The object of public admiration will invariably be the object of the wishes of individuals, and if one has to be rich in order to shine then being rich will always be the dominant passion." Fortunately for legislators, it was possible to mitigate this problem by erecting alternative objects of public admiration. By instituting ceremonies, displays, and titles, it was possible "to change the objects of this luxury, and so render its example less pernicious." Despite being man-made, public displays and ceremonies would go far in altering the natural course of public sentiment: "It is hard to exaggerate the extent to which the people's heart follows its eyes and how impressed it is with the majesty of ceremonials." Imposing visual attractions could be counted on to "convey magnificence with men rather than with things." As Adams would later do, Rousseau pointed to the Roman republic as an example of a political community that understood the use of pomp and ceremony for counterbalancing the esteem of wealth: "The Consuls of Rome were often very poor, but they had their lictors, and plebeians attained the Consulship." Not only did the Romans dignify offices that could compete with wealth, they also denigrated the status of wealth by associating luxury with the plight of vanquished enemies. "The captive Kings," Rousseau wrote, "were shackled with chains of gold and precious stones." Such spectacles gave Romans a correct understanding of luxury. When luxury was associated with dishonor, it lost its allure. It continued to sparkle, but "the more brilliant it was, the less it was seductive."[32]

Much like Rousseau, Adams believed that titles could function as alternative objects of public sentiment that would direct public admiration away from wealth. It was not that sympathy and admiration for wealth could be entirely extinguished, or that honorific titles could altogether replace the honor accorded to wealth. Rather, the aim was to create a plurality of honors such that no single quality—whether it be wealth, strength, intelligence, or any other advantage—could monopolize public sympathy. He was not entirely confident that the strategy would succeed, and in his retirement-era letters to Benjamin Rush he lamented the failure of the effort to use military decorations as an alternative to wealth. "Military honors have excited ambition to struggle against avarice, till military honors have degenerated into hereditary dignities."[33] Nonetheless, in an American nation growing increasingly "bedollared," there was no alternative: "Former ages have never discovered any remedy against the universal gangrene of avarice in commercial countries but setting up ambition as a rival to it."[34]

If the full force of Adams's argument for titles went unappreciated by his critics, this was because they were predisposed to dismiss titles as chimerical relics of the pre-republican world. In *Rights of Man*, Thomas Paine equated titles with the ribbons and garters of children. A title like "duke" or "count" signified nothing of meaning. Without describing any quality of character, such a title was like a cheap nickname that "marks a sort of foppery in the human character." If the idea of rank or dignity were to have any meaning in a republican order, it would have to be associated with real human qualities: "It must now take the substantial ground of character, instead of the chimerical ground of titles." Reasoning from a state of nature—from an imagined time when man first came "from the hand of his Maker"—Paine concluded that man in his original state carried only the title of "man." "Man was his high and only title, and a higher cannot be given him."[35]

As Senator William Maclay insisted, America had undergone a profound and widespread shift of sentiment regarding public distinctions. In recent years there had been "a revolution in the sentiments of people respecting government equally great as that which had happened in the Government itself." Having emerged from "a hard struggle for our liberty against kingly authority," wrote Maclay, "the minds of men are still heated" and "everything related to that species of government is odious to the people." Words like "highness," an appellation attached to German princes, "would have a most ungrateful sound to many thousands of industrious citizens who had fled from German oppression." In light of the revolution of sentiment, all historical precedent was irrelevant. It mattered not that Rome, Sparta, and so many civilizations had instituted dignified offices, for "mankind now considered themselves as little bound to imitate the follies of civilized nations as the brutalities of savages."[36]

Like Paine, Maclay spoke not merely for public sentiments but for an emergent democratic ideology. He proclaimed that in the past two decades alone "more light had been thrown on the subject of governments and on human affairs in general than for several generations before," and that "this light of knowledge had diminished the veneration for titles." The true philosophers of government and human affairs admitted only the necessity— and not the utility—of government, and they endeavored "to correct the vices and expose the follies which have been ingrafted upon it." Furthermore, those reflecting on government sought "to reduce the practice of it to the principles of common sense, such as we see exemplified by the merchant, the mechanic, and the farmer."[37] If government was nothing other than the simple instrument of the people, what reason was there to distinguish its officeholder from the common citizenry?

What was missing in Maclay's critique—and what was missing in the broader ideological assault on honorific titles—was any recognition of the powerful distinctions of wealth that would naturally emerge from the formally free and equal conditions of the commercial republic. Adams differed from his contemporaries in his insistence that wealth could distinguish individuals as readily as formal titles and that those persons distinguished by wealth would enjoy the admiration and sympathy of the public.

He took pains to point out that certain oligarchic sentiments—namely, sympathy and admiration for the wealthiest citizens—would be a potent source of oligarchic power. Adams's detractors have been correct to label him a critic of democracy, but they have missed what was perhaps his most compelling line of criticism. In the end, Adams's most powerful critique of the democratic revolution was that it knocked down all pillars of distinction except for one. "Are riches," he asked, "to be the only distinction? Is there any distinction more degrading than riches?"[38]

Let Distinction Counteract Distinction

American democracy has, in practice, often achieved something like a pluralism of honors. Whether or not most Founding Era Americans intended it to be so, honorific societies abound in America. Some are the creatures of government, such as the National Endowment for the Arts, which doles out lifetime achievement awards to novelists, actors, singers, and poets. Honors are also created and distributed by such private organizations as the MacArthur Fellows Program, the National Baseball Hall of Fame, and the Academy Awards. Perhaps most important, certain high public offices continue to carry a great deal of esteem. Generals and Supreme Court justices, and to a lesser extent governors and senators, still enjoy a degree of honorific status by virtue of the offices they occupy. And though we do not call our president "highness" or "excellency," we do invest a great deal of honorary significance in the trappings of the office. Air Force One, the White House, the Oval Office—all of these iconic symbols grant the presidency a certain grandeur that Adams would likely have endorsed.

Moreover, the sheer vastness and diversity of American culture seems to all but guarantee a multiplicity of honors. If there were ever a danger in America of wealth monopolizing public esteem, this danger seems amply checked by America's diversity of subcultures, each with its own unique markers of distinction. Observing 1960s America, the novelist Tom Wolfe pointed out that the culture was so splintered—with the status symbols of each subculture so unique—that one regional or ethnic group could hardly recognize the status symbols of the other. The professional journalist of the Northeast, for example, could hardly comprehend the esteem that the "good old boy" of rural North Carolina attached to professional stock-car racing; and the good old boy, in turn, would find puzzling the esteem that so many Puerto Rican New Yorkers accorded to the professional wrestler Antonino Rocca.[39] James Madison predicted that the bigness of America would guarantee the presence of so many competing factions that a single passion or interest could not dominate the rest. He might have added that this same dynamic would prevent the predominance of any single object of public sympathy.

And yet, if there remain certain checks on our oligarchic passions, there also remain causes for concern. First, the United States is currently on a trajectory of increasing income inequality and an ever-growing concentration of wealth. It could be that as the rich get richer, and as the social distance between the rich and the non-rich continues to yawn, wealth will loom larger vis-à-vis competing markers of distinction and will therefore attract more and more public sympathy. It should be noted that John Adams's fears of growing sympathy for the rich took place in the context of rapidly increasing economic inequality.[40] Likewise, it is relevant to point out that Thorsten Veblen—the American thinker who, after Adams, wrote most incisively about oligarchic passions—did so in the context of the Gilded Age, an era of wealth concentration that is rivaled in American history only by our current period of inequality.

A second cause for concern is that even if our institutions have, in practice, often worked to restrain sympathy for the rich, modern democratic ideologies have not appreciated the counter-oligarchic role of honorifics. The modern democratic citizen is embarrassed by honorific titles. "I am ashamed," wrote Ralph Waldo Emerson in his most famous essay, "to think how easily we capitulate to badges and names."[41] It is a widely shared suspicion, after all, that there is something profoundly undemocratic about granting honor to distinguished individuals. It seems that in a democracy what should be honored is not the distinctive qualities of a select few but the common humanity of all. In other words, there is an ethic of *human* dignity that seems to oppose the elite forms of dignity that Adams defended.[42] Moreover, in America there has long been an instinctive democratic impulse—perhaps most clearly traceable to Jacksonian ideology—that opposes the attachment of honors to public offices on the grounds that such honors elevate offices *above* the station of the common citizen. It is such an impulse that in part motivates the calls for strict limits on the duration and number of legislative terms and that calls for the election, rather than the appointment, of judges.

The ideological aversion to honorific titles is especially pronounced when it comes to the role of the state in determining what, specifically, is honorable. Why should the state meddle in matters of prestige and esteem? Are not such matters better dealt with by the people themselves? When the economist Thomas Piketty was recently chosen by the French government to join the Legion of Honor, he promptly declined. Piketty, the social scientist who has done more than any other to lay bare the extent of inequality and the specter of oligarchy in the United States and other advanced democracies, announced that the government should focus on economic policy rather than attempt "to decide who is honorable."[43]

But Adams's writings suggest the possibility that in the absence of honorific titles, the modern commercial republic is vulnerable to oligarchic passions and, therefore, to domination by the rich.[44] As Adams pointed out, if no formal dignities are permitted, if all artificial distinctions are abolished, the result will not be the nonexistence of distinction. Instead, there will be only one distinction that will remain: that of wealth. The likes of Paine and Maclay would inform us that we must choose between a titled aristocracy and a plain democracy. Adams suggested that we face a different choice: a choice between an oligarchic democracy and a dignified democracy. An oligarchic democracy results when a democratic society fails to make collective decisions about what to honor. Against its own democratic intentions, such a society empowers those qualities that naturally garner the sympathies of the public: birth, beauty, and especially wealth. A dignified democracy, by contrast, would be a democracy in which distinction is made to counteract distinction. It would be a democracy in which honors are attached to a variety of stations and pursuits. Sympathy for the rich would survive in such a democracy, but one would not need to fear oligarchy.

American Oligarchy?

Among the new objects that attracted my attention
during my stay in the United States, none struck my
eye more vividly than the equality of conditions.

—ALEXIS DE TOCQUEVILLE,
Democracy in America

The War that is now breaking out will render our
Country, whether she is forced into it, or not, rich, great
and powerful in comparison of what she now is, and
Riches Grandeur and Power will have the same effect
upon American as it has upon European minds.

—JOHN ADAMS TO THOMAS JEFFERSON,
9 October 1787

SOME HAVE SUGGESTED THAT Adams's obsession with inequality stemmed from a wounded psyche. John Howe's
classic *The Changing Political Thought of John Adams*, written a
half century ago, traced Adams's worry about the widening
chasm between the haves and have-nots to his shifting fortunes
as a political leader. From the time when Adams began contemplating writing the *Defence*, "a correspondence developed between the satisfactions of his own life—his early years as a confident political leader, successful in his ambitions and applauded
by the people—and his outlook on American society." As his

own popularity spoiled, so too did his estimation of the American people. Likewise, other scholars traced Adams's obsession with the rich to his well-known vanity. Could it be that his obsession with wealth was ultimately an expression of status anxiety, the envy of an aging statesman witnessing the rising prestige of a new commercial elite?

This book has traced Adams's fear of oligarchy to a more rational source. I have argued that Adams was a practical political scientist who concluded through his studies and experiences that republican governments had always been threatened by elite domination and that America would be no different.

I have suggested that Adams deserves to be remembered not just as a statesman but also as a shrewd critic of oligarchy. In the American intellectual tradition he should be understood as a predecessor to Alexis de Tocqueville, the purveyor of a "new science of politics," who would arrive in America from France just a few years after Adams's death. Much as Tocqueville later would, Adams sought to make sense of American politics not just by comprehending its formal institutions but also by discerning its complex psychological character. In important respects Adams stands as the converse, or mirror image, to Tocqueville. Whereas Tocqueville's subject was American democracy, Adams's was American oligarchy. Tocqueville, an aristocrat, was awed by the spirit of equality that pervaded America. Adams, who had sprung from plebeian origins, observed the ills of inequality in Europe and doubted that America would escape them. Tocqueville worried that the democratic revolution would eventually snuff out individual liberty. Adams's concern was that the democratic revolution would, paradoxically, enable new forms of oligarchic power to go unchecked.

Adams's critics insisted that his worries were unfounded. "We have no such thing as orders, ranks, or nobility," noted John Stevens, and "it is almost impossible they should ever gain any footing here." Real aristocracy would require a concentration of wealth in a few hands—an unlikely outcome in nation where "there is little danger to be apprehended from this source of wealth being confined to a few places, or to a few persons" and where wealth "in all probability . . . will be diffused everywhere."[2] Roger Sherman argued similarly that Adams's idea of aristocracy was obsolete in light of the structure of American political institutions: "As both branches of Congress are eligible from the citizens at large, and wealth is not a requisite qualification, both will commonly be composed of members of similar circumstances in life." Because wealth is decoupled from officeholding under the new Constitution, Sherman argued, there are "no principles in our constitution that have any tendency to aristocracy."[3]

From the very beginning, Adams's contemporaries presented arguments that would later be associated with the idea of American exceptionalism—the notion that the United States, with its fluid society and free institutions, altogether lacks the class divisions of more rigidly stratified societies. Equality, Charles Pinckney announced at the Federal Convention, was the "leading feature" of the United States. With every freeman granted "a right to the same protection and security" and with each enjoying an equal power both to vote and to attain the highest offices, America was uniquely free of the formal class distinctions that characterized the Old World. Riches were not concentrated in the hands of a few but instead "in the great body of the people, among whom there are no men of wealth, and very few of real poverty." There were neither few nor many in America, but rather "one great & equal body of citizens . . . among whom there are no distinctions of rank, and very few or none of fortune."[4]

Tocqueville would later canonize this notion, observing that the New England colonies, peopled as they were by members of England's puritanical middle class, lacked the hierarchical social divisions of the mother country and offered to the world "the new spectacle of a society homogeneous in all its parts."[5] Furthermore, wealth in America had been detached from territory, thereby undermining pretensions to aristocratic status among America's rich.[6] In the twentieth century, Louis Hartz influentially dismissed the idea of an American aristocracy as a false imposition of European social categories on an entirely different, exceptional United States. Nothing resembling the European struggle between the bourgeoisie and the nobility had ever occurred in America. American society was "bourgeois" through and through, altogether lacking the neo-feudal, hierarchical class structure of European monarchies. Indeed, Americans were (and are) "a kind of national embodiment of the concept of the bourgeoisie."[7]

Adams was perhaps the first critic of the idea of American exceptionalism. It was a fantasy to believe that aristocratic power would recede with the abolition of hereditary privilege. The power of wealth—like the power of birth and beauty—was not a mere byproduct of Old World institutions. Oligarchic power was, at least in part, a reflection of human nature. To his critics, who did not comprehend how a corrupt phenomenon could be called natural, Adams could reply that human nature itself was, to a degree, corrupt. As Reinhold Niebuhr observed, Adams had the mind of a realist—a disposition that made him immune to the type of innocence that led Jefferson to believe that social and economic freedom would naturally generate political equality.[8]

Americans, swept up in the promise of their singularity, seemed inclined to neglect altogether their propensity for oligarchy. But there were plentiful signs in Adams's America that oligarchic tendencies remained in spite of the democratization of formal institutions. Adams believed that it was urgent that Americans recognize this fact, for "Know thyself" was not merely an individual command but a collective one. The injunction to examine oneself honestly and without pretense was, Adams insisted, "as useful a precept to nations as to men."[9]

Is today's United States closer to Tocqueville's or to Adams's? It is undoubtedly true that our society still bears a resemblance to the rambunctious democracy described by Tocqueville. Despite the gaping inequality we observe in income and wealth, America is still a place where there exists a certain equality of ambition. A foreign observer would likely be struck today, as Tocqueville was in the age of Jackson, by the restlessness of Americans and "the innumerable multitude of those who seek to get out of their original condition."[10] And if we do in fact sympathize with the rich, as Adams predicted we would, it is surely also true that we scoff at anyone who expects our deference. Even if the rich enjoy special sympathy, few Americans would argue that they *deserve* it. As Tocqueville observed, even if we do not demand that the rich sacrifice their money, we do insist that they sacrifice their pride. If Americans admire wealth, they detest snobbery.[11]

And yet, if we still observe aspects of what Tocqueville described as an exceptional "equality of conditions," today it appears that the United States has grown exceptional in its *inequality* of conditions. Gone are the days of the nineteenth-century frontier, when, as Tocqueville described, "land costs little and each man easily becomes a property owner."[12] And since 1980, we have observed a steady erosion of the American middle class that grew out of the broad-based economic growth of the mid-twentieth century. Thomas Piketty has noted that in terms of income inequality, today's United States might be more unequal than "any other society at any time in the past, anywhere in the world."[13] Perhaps most important of all, it increasingly appears that rising inequality has been accompanied by an unraveling of the social fabric, and with it the Tocquevillian ideal of a dem-

ocratic community that binds the opulent and the ordinary together in relations of reciprocity. As Charles Murray has observed, inequality has led us to a point in which "the people who
have so much influence on the course of the nation have little
direct experience with the lives of ordinary Americans, and make
their judgments about what's good for other people based on
their own highly atypical lives."[14]

If, in fact, we are living not just with Tocqueville's democracy,
but also with Adams's oligarchy, what then? The first step toward
tending to our oligarchic malady, perhaps, is admitting that we
are not exceptionally immune. As Adams put it so plainly and
truthfully: "There is no special providence for Americans, and
their nature is the same with that of others."[15]

$\mathcal{N}otes$

INTRODUCTION

1. Adams to Jefferson, 13 July 1813, *The Adams-Jefferson Letters: The Complete Correspondence between Thomas Jefferson and Abigail and John Adams*, ed. Lester J. Cappon (Chapel Hill: University of North Carolina Press, 1987).

2. Gordon S. Wood, *The Creation of the American Republic: 1776–1787* (Chapel Hill: University of North Carolina Press, 1998), 568.

3. Arthur Lovejoy, *Reflections on Human Nature* (Baltimore: Johns Hopkins Press, 1961), 34. Zoltán Haraszti recalled Harold Laski's estimation of Adams as having been "the greatest political thinker whom America has yet produced." See Haraszti, *John Adams and the Prophets of Progress* (Cambridge, MA: Harvard University Press, 1952). Vernon Louis Parrington called Adams "the most notable thinker—with the possible exception of John C. Calhoun—among American statesmen." See Parrington, *The Colonial Mind, 1600–1800* (New York, 1927), 320.

4. Adams to Jefferson, 13 July 1813, *Adams-Jefferson Letters*.

5. Ibid.

6. Thomas Jefferson, *Writings*, ed. Merrill Peterson (New York: Library of America, 1984), 671.

7. Adams to Jefferson, 13 July 1813, *Adams-Jefferson Letters*.

8. In the final chapter of the *Discourses*, Adams refers to the common American citizenry as "We, the Plebeians." See John Adams, *The Works of John Adams, Second President of the United States*, 10 vols., ed. Charles Francis Adams (Boston: Little, Brown, 1850–56), 6: 395 (hereafter, *Works*). For an

account of Adams's lineage and upbringing, see Page Smith, *John Adams*, vol. 1, *1735–1784* (Garden City: Doubleday & Company, 1962), 1–14. As Oscar Handlin and Mary Flug Handlin note in their study of the political economy of late-eighteenth- and early-nineteenth-century Massachusetts, Adams's varied background made him uniquely suited to republican politics: "A product of agricultural Braintree, linked to the professional classes by training and interests, he spent his youth in frontier Worcester and gathered his political experience in the turbulent politics of Suffolk County. A varied career, residence in the west and in the east, gave him a sympathetic understanding of the diverse elements of his society, unmatched by any of his contemporaries." See Handlin and Handlin, *Commonwealth: A Study of the Role of Government in the American Economy: Massachusetts, 1774–1861* (Cambridge, MA: Belknap Press of Harvard University Press), 28.

9. See George C. Homans, "John Adams and the Constitution of Massachusetts," *Proceedings of the American Philosophical Society* 125, no. 4 (1981): 286–291.

10. *The American Annual Register; for the Years 1825–6*, ed. Joseph Blunt (New York: G & C Carvill, 1827), 30.

11. As Danielle Allen has observed, Adams was what we today call a politico, a master of backroom strategizing and deal making. See Allen, *Our Declaration: A Reading of the Declaration of Independence in Defense of Equality* (New York: W. W. Norton & Company, 2014), chap. 6.

12. *Works* 2: 59.

13. John Adams to Abigail Adams, 12 May 1780, *The Adams Papers: Adams Family Correspondence*, ed. L. H. Butterfield and Marc Friedlander (Cambridge, MA: Belknap Press of Harvard University Press, 1973), vol. 3.

14. *Journal of Debates and Proceedings in the Convention of Delegates Chosen to Revise the Constitution of Massachusetts* (Bos-

ton: The Office of the Daily Advertiser, 1821), 134. Citing this episode, Sean Wilentz refers to Adams as an "anti-majoritarian." See Wilentz, *The Rise of American Democracy: Jefferson to Lincoln* (New York: W. W. Norton, 2005), 187–88.

15. *Works*, 6: 9.

16. See Page Smith, *John Adams*, vol. 1, *1735–1784*, 121–23.

17. *Works*, 3: 451–56.

18. Ibid., 3: 463–64.

19. Ibid., 3: 456. When Adams described a class of men seeking to reintroduce canon and feudal law, he likely had in mind his fellow members of the Massachusetts bar, most of whom sided with the crown in the controversies of the Revolutionary era. For a thorough background of the eighteenth-century development of the Massachusetts legal community and Adams's place therein, see John M. Murrin, "The Legal Transformation: The Bench and Bar of Eighteenth-Century Massachusetts," in *Colonial America: Essays in Politics and Social Development*, ed. Stanley N. Katz (Boston: Little, Brown, 1971).

20. Adams to Jefferson, 13 July 1813, *Adams-Jefferson Letters*.

21. Adams to Jefferson, 9 July 1813, ibid.

22. See especially *Republic of Plato*, trans. Allan Bloom (New York: Basic Books, 1991), 550c2–552e5; Aristotle, *Politics and the Constitution of Athens*, ed. Stephen Everson (Cambridge, MA: Cambridge University Press, 1996), 1279b20–1280a6, 1290b2, 1292a21–31, 1301a26–b14, 1307a6–28, 1309b38–1310a5; Polybius, *The Histories*, vol. 3, *Books 5–8*, trans. W. R. Paton, rev. F. W. Walbank and Christian Habicht (Cambridge, MA: Harvard University Press, 2011), bk. 6: viii, x.

23. My analysis is indebted to John McCormick's critique of the class-anonymous descriptions of the people found in the writings of James Madison and other republican theorists. See McCormick, *Machiavellian Democracy* (Cambridge: Cambridge University Press, 2011), 16–17.

24. C. Wright Mills, *The Power Elite* (Oxford: Oxford University Press, 2000); Judith Shklar, *Redeeming American Political Thought* (Chicago: University of Chicago Press, 1998).

25. Joyce Appleby, *Liberalism and Republicanism in the Historical Imagination* (Cambridge, MA: Harvard University Press, 1992), 200.

26. Russell Kirk, *The Conservative Mind: From Burke to Eliot*, 7th rev. ed. (Washington, DC: Regnery, 1985), 89.

27. Hannah Arendt, *On Revolution* (New York: Viking, 1963), 119; J.G.A. Pocock, *The Machiavellian Moment: Florentine Political Thought and the Atlantic Republican Tradition* (Princeton, NJ: Princeton University Press, 1975), 526. Picking up on this line of interpretation, Bruce Miroff has explored in detail Adams's understanding of the love of fame as a political motivation and his ideas about how republics might "encourage and reward the desire for fame through symbolic honors, while using its energies to serve the public good." I discuss this facet of Adams's thought at length in chapter 4. See Miroff, "Merit, Fame, and Political Leadership," *Journal of Politics* 48, no. 1 (1986): 116–32.

28. C. Bradley Thompson, *John Adams and the Spirit of Liberty* (Lawrence: University Press of Kansas, 1998), 165, 220.

29. Wood, *Creation of the American Republic*, 592. Joseph J. Ellis has made this same point about Wood's analysis in *Passionate Sage: The Character and Legacy of John Adams* (New York: W. W. Norton & Company, 2001), 261.

30. R. R. Palmer, *The Age of the Democratic Revolution: A Political History of Europe and America, 1760–1800* (Princeton, NJ: Princeton University Press, 1970), 272.

31. Shklar, *Redeeming American Political Thought*, 148, 156.

32. Ellis, *Passionate Sage*, 153, 156, 160.

33. John Ferling, *John Adams: A Life* (Oxford: Oxford University Press, 1992), 424, 452.

34. John Patrick Diggins, *John Adams* (New York: Times Books, 2003), 167, 168, 169.

35. For evidence of the responsiveness of American political institutions to affluent voters, see Martin Gilens, *Affluence and Influence* (Princeton, NJ: Princeton University Press, 2012); and Larry M. Bartels, *Unequal Democracy: The Political Economy of the New Gilded Age* (Princeton, NJ: Princeton University Press, 2008). For a discussion of the influence of the superrich in modern democracies, see Jeffrey Winters, *Oligarchy* (Cambridge: Cambridge University Press, 2012), chap. 5. To a striking degree, even the political behavior of ordinary voters appears to track the agendas and pet projects of wealthy individuals. For a discussion of the coincidence between the voting behavior of the public and preferences of the rich, see "Homer Gets a Tax Cut," in Bartels, *Unequal Democracy*, chap. 6.

36. For compelling accounts of the influence of money in the electoral and lobbying arenas, see Jacob S. Hacker and Paul Pierson, *Winner-Take-All Politics: How Washington Made the Rich Richer—And Turned Its Back on the Middle Class* (New York: Simon & Schuster, 2010); and Kay Lehman Schlozman, Sidney Verba, Henry E. Brady, *The Unheavenly Chorus: Unequal Political Voice and the Broken Promise of American Democracy* (Princeton, NJ: Princeton University Press, 2012). For an account of the capacity of the rich to gain influence by shaping public opinion, see G. William Domhoff, *Who Rules America? Power and Politics*, Fourth Edition (Boston: McGraw Hill, 2002), chap. 4. For a description of the modern "income defense industry," see Winters, *Oligarchy*, chap. 5.

37. Joseph S. Nye, Jr. *Soft Power: The Means to Success in World Politics* (New York: Public Affairs Books, 2004), x.

38. Adam Smith, *The Theory of Moral Sentiments*, ed. D. D. Raphael and A. L. Macfie (Indianapolis: Liberty Fund, 1976), 52.

39. *Works*, 4: 392.

40. Ibid., 4: 444–45.

41. John Rawls, *Political Liberalism* (New York: Columbia University Press, 1996), 327.

42. Michael Walzer, *Spheres of Justice: A Defense of Pluralism and Equality* (New York: Basic Books, 1983), 17–19.

43. Michael Walzer, "Liberalism and the Art of Separation," *Political Theory* 12, no. 3 (1984), 318.

44. Cass R. Sunstein, "Political Equality and Unintended Consequences," *Columbia Law Review* 94, no. 4 (1994), 1390.

45. Jean-Jacques Rousseau, *The Social Contract*, trans. Maurice Cranston (New York: Penguin Books, 1968): bk. 2, chap. 11.

46. Domhoff, *Who Rules America?*, chap. 4.

47. Recent works on the disproportionate lobbying power of organizations representing big business and the rich include and Hacker and Pierson, *Winner-Take-All Politics:* and Schlozman, Verba, Brady, *The Unheavenly Chorus*.

48. Winters describes the workings of the "income defense industry" in the United States in *Oligarchy*, chap. 5.

49. Samuel P. Huntington, *American Politics: The Promise of Disharmony* (Cambridge, MA: Harvard University Press, 1981), 38.

50. Haraszti, *John Adams and the Prophets of Progress*, 230.

Chapter One: A Perennial Problem

1. John Milton Niles, *Speech on the Bill Imposing Additional Duties, as Depositaries in Certain Cases, on Public Officers, &c.* (Washington, DC: Globe Office, 1838).

2. Melancton Smith, 21 June 1788, in *The Complete Anti-Federalist*, 7 vols., ed. Herbert J. Storing (Chicago: University of Chicago Press, 1981), 6: 157–59; Brutus, letter 3, in ibid., 2: 381.

3. See James Madison, *Writings* (New York: Library of America, 1999), 160–67. According to Max Farrand's classic account of the Federal Convention, "Madison's ideas were the predominating factor in the framing of the Constitution." See Farrand, *The Framing of the Constitution* (New Haven, CT: Yale University Press, 1913), 196–98.

4. See Palmer, *The Age of the Democratic Revolution*, 267.

5. Melancton Smith, 21 June 1788, in *Complete Anti-Federalist*, 6: 157–59.

6. Hamilton, speech of 21 June 1788, *Papers of Alexander Hamilton*, vol. 5, ed. Harold C. Syrett and Jacob E. Cooke (New York: Columbia University Press, 1962).

7. Months earlier he had expressed a number of criticisms of the system but concluded in a letter to John Jay that "a result of accommodation and compromise cannot be supposed perfectly to coincide with everyone's ideas of perfection," and that "the public mind cannot be occupied about a nobler object than the proposed plan of government." *The Works of John Adams, Second President of the United States*, 10 vols., ed. Charles Francis Adams (Boston: Little, Brown, 1850–56), 8: 467.

8. Melancton Smith, 23 June 1788, in *Complete Anti-Federalist*, 6: 162. There is some evidence supporting the view that Melancton Smith was the writer behind the pseudonyms Brutus and The Federal Farmer, the two pseudonymous writers who, more than any others, appear to take after John Adams in their views of natural aristocracy. See Michael Zuckert and Derek A. Webb, introduction, in *Anti-Federalist Writings of the Melancton Smith Circle*, ed. Michael Zuckert and Derek A. Webb (Indianapolis: Liberty Fund, 2009). In his classic commentary on Anti-Federalist thought, Herbert Storing briefly discussed the similarity between Adams and the Anti-Federalists on the issue of aristocracy. Storing quoted at length A [Maryland] Farmer on the problem of

aristocratic power: "In fine, in all governments by *representation* or *delegation of power*, where property is secured by fixed and permanent laws, from the rage of the populace on one side, and the tyranny of a despot on the other, the aristocracy will and must rule; that is a number of the wealthiest individuals, and the heads of great families:—The perfection of all political wisdom is to temper this aristocracy as to prevent oppression." Herbert J. Storing, *What the Anti-Federalists Were* For (Chicago: University of Chicago Press, 1981), 57–58.

9. Mills, *The Power Elite*, 89–93.

10. Shklar, *Redeeming American Political Thought*, chap. 10. As I have noted in the introduction, several other scholars have appreciated Adams's preoccupation with socioeconomic elites. See especially Ellis, *Passionate Sage*, 149–65; John Diggins, *John Adams*, 167–69; Thompson, *John Adams and the Spirit of Liberty*, 165, 220.

11. Madison to Jefferson, 6 June 1987, *The Papers of Thomas Jefferson*, vol. 11, *January 1787 to August 1787*, ed. Julian P. Boyd (Princeton, NJ: Princeton University Press, 1959), 401–2.

12. Rev. James Madison to James Madison, 11 June 1787, *Proceedings of the Massachusetts Historical Society*, 2nd ser., 17 (1903): 465. For an account of the early reception of Adams's *Defence* in America, see Wood, *Creation of the American Republic*, chap. 14.

13. M. Turgot, "Extract of a Letter of M. Turgot to Dr. Richard Price," in *Works*, 4: 279.

14. *Works*, 4: 299–300.

15. The similar idea of the mixed constitution can be traced back through earlier writings including those of Aristotle, Plato, and Thucydides. But the idea of a constitution that balances social forces against each other is quite different than the older idea of a constitution that combines competing principles of justice.

16. Polybius, *The Histories*, 6.10.1–11.

17. The theory first gained popularity following a public address by Charles I issued in June 1642 just months before the outbreak of the Civil War. The *Answer to the Nineteen Propositions* rejected the Long Parliament's demands for concessions of political power on the grounds that such concessions would upset the balance between king, the Lords, and the Commons that characterized the English constitution. The king's powers were not to be justified in terms of divine right but in Polybian terms of equilibrium: institutions representing society's one, few, and many needed to be empowered to check one another in order to prevent domination by any single element. The application of the classical theory continued through to the late eighteenth century, as British writers, including William Blackstone, William Paley, and Edmund Burke, continued to use the language of "balance" to describe and defend British institutions. See Corinne Comstock Weston, *English Constitutional Theory and the House of Lords: 1556–1832* (New York: Columbia University Press, 1965), 123–37.

18. For a discussion of Montesquieu's role in broadcasting the English idea of balanced government to an international audience, see ibid., 123–26.

19. Montesquieu, *The Spirit of the Laws*, trans. Anne M. Cohler, Basia C. Miller, and Harold S. Stone (Cambridge: Cambridge University Press, 1989), bk. 11, chap. 6. On Montesquieu's influence in England, see Weston, *English Constitutional Theory*, 128–29. For a discussion on the unique combination of the idea of balanced government with the idea of the separation of powers in Montesquieu's thought, see M.J.C. Vile, *Constitutionalism and the Separation of Powers* (Oxford: Oxford University Press, 1967), chap. 4. Also see Richard Bellamy, "The Political Form of the Constitution: The

Separation of Powers, Rights, and Representative Democracy," *Political Studies* 44 (1996): 436–456.

20. Vile, *Constitutionalism*, 184.

21. *Works*, 4: 358. For accounts of the influence of De Lolme's work, see Palmer, *Age of the Democratic Revolution*, 145; and Weston, *English Constitutional Theory*, 128–31. For an assessment of De Lolme's influence on Adams, see Appleby, *Liberalism and Republicanism*, 194–202.

22. Vile, *Constitutionalism*, 184.

23. Kinch Hoekstra, a scholar of seventeenth-century absolutism, provides a clarifying example of the peril that divided sovereignty was thought to entail: "It is worse than fruitless to give the right or power of raising revenue to one body and the right or power of the military to another—far from leading to a happy balance, the military will fail without revenue, and without the military no revenue can be raised. If they remain separated, both rights are worthless, both powers powerless. As soon as it is divided, sovereignty is destroyed." See Hoekstra, "Early Modern Absolutism and Constitutionalism," *Cardozo Law Review* 34 (2012–2013): 1081. According to Hobbes, the idea of a division of legislative authority stood against the essence of a commonwealth. "For what is it to divide the Power of a Common-wealth," Hobbes asked, "but to Dissolve it; for Powers divided mutually destroy each other." Hobbes, *Leviathan*, ed. Richard Tuck (Cambridge: Cambridge University Press, 1996), 225.

24. See Palmer, *Age of the Democratic Revolution*, 67–74.

25. Rousseau, *The Social Contract*, bk. 2, chap. 2. Rousseau insisted that laws, in order to serve as generally applicable rules, had to emanate from the general will of the entire community. There was no separate role for "the one" or "the few"—or the king or House of Lords—in legislation. It is

important to note that Rousseau did not think it impossible or unwise to divide the powers of *government* into different parts. Rousseau distinguished the division of government—the executive organ of the state—from the division of sovereignty, or legislative power. See bk. 3, especially chaps. 1 and 7.

26. Madison said that if there was a single criterion that distinguished republican governments from other forms, it was the popular derivation of all offices. See Madison, *Writings*, 212.

27. As Madison wrote, the American system was uniquely "unmixed" in its design. Madison, *Writings*, 169. "Mixed" and "balanced" are terms that have historically been used somewhat interchangeably to describe models of government that embody the parts of society in political institutions.

28. See Martin Diamond, "Democracy and the Federalist: A Reconstruction of the Framers' Intent," *American Political Science Review* 53, no. 1 (1959), 59–60.

29. Alexander Hamilton, James Madison, and John Jay, *The Federalist, no. 69*, ed. T. Ball (Cambridge: Cambridge University Press, 2003), 340.

30. Ibid., no. 70, 341–42; for an account of the Federalists' unique justifications of the Senate and the president during the ratification debates, see Wood, *The Creation of the American Republic*, 543–62.

31. John Stevens, *Observations on Government, Including Some Animadversions on Mr. Adams's Defence of the Constitutions of Government of the United States of America: and on Mr. De Lolme's Constitution of England* (New York: W. Ross, 1787).

32. James Madison sent a copy to Philip Mazzei, an Italian physician and member of Thomas Jefferson's social circle in Paris. Mazzei then forwarded the pamphlet to Condorcet

and Dupont. See Appleby, *Liberalism and Republicanism*, 243.

33. Quoted in Appleby, *Liberalism and Republicanism*, 249. My account of the influence of Stevens's pamphlet on the Constituent Assembly is drawn from ibid., 243–50 and Palmer, *Age of Democratic Revolution*, 279–82.

34. Quoted in Appleby, *Liberalism and Republicanism*, 248.

35. Quoted in David McCullough, *John Adams* (New York: Simon & Schuster, 2001), 373.

36. Abigail Adams to John Quincy Adams, 26 March 1787, Adams, *The Adams Papers*, vol. 8.

37. "From John Adams to Benjamin Franklin, 27 January 1787," Founders Online, National Archives (http://founders.archives.gov/documents/Adams/99–02–02–0026 [last update: 2015–12–30]).

38. *Works*, 4: 290. In *Thoughts on Government*, written a decade before the *Defence*, Adams had followed the traditional British conception of political struggle as between the chief magistrate and the people. Echoing theories of balanced government going back to Polybius, Adams viewed the aristocratic part, sitting in an upper house, "as a mediator between the two extreme branches of the legislature, that which represents the people, and that which is vested with the executive power." Only a separate legislative body constituted by aristocrats could guard against the tyranny of an overweening people or an omnipotent executive. See *Works*, 4: 195–96.

39. *Works*, 4: 290–91. For accounts of Adams's Senate as an ostracizing body, see Palmer, *Age of the Democratic Revolution*, 274; and Wood, *Creation of the American Republic*, 576–78. It should be noted that the "ostracism" Adams described was much less severe than the classical Athenian practice of expulsion. Both practices were intended to neutralize the

threat posed by certain citizens. But rather than expelling the ambitious, Adams's form of ostracism would trap them within government and utilize their talents.

40. In addition to defending a dignified executive in the *Defence*, Adams notoriously defended presidential titles in a heated debate on the Senate floor in the opening weeks of the new national government. Presiding in his role as president of the Senate, Adams adamantly weighed in on the issue of how the president was to be addressed, insisting on a dignified title for the president and stubbornly resisting opposition even as his initial allies conceded the issue. By the time the matter was resolved in favor of the simple title "president of the United States," Adams had alienated many of his peers and had even managed to lose the confidence of President Washington. The episode would be related time and again by future historians as proof of Adams's partiality to royal authority. For an extended account of this episode, see Smith, *John Adams*, vol. 2, *1784–1826*, 747–58. I discuss the titles debate in more detail in chap. 4 of this book.

41. *Works*, 4: 358. For accounts of the influence of De Lolme's work, see Palmer, *Age of the Democratic Revolution*, 145; and Weston, *English Constitutional Theory*, 128–31. For an assessment of De Lolme's influence on Adams, see Appleby, "New Republican Synthesis," 583–90. The likely influence of De Lolme's *Constitution* on Adams's *Defence* has been either overlooked or misunderstood, as interpreters have attributed to De Lolme a conservative, traditional theory of the British constitution. Joyce Appleby, who has documented Adams's indebtedness to De Lolme, reads De Lolme as the source of Adams's aristocratic commitments. Meanwhile, C. Bradley Thompson, who has done more than any other scholar to defend Adams's writings from charges of reactionary conservatism, has downplayed the influence of "conservative

Anglophiles like Jean De Lolme." Thompson, *John Adams and the Spirit of Liberty*, 92, 245. Both Appleby and Thompson missed the extent to which De Lolme's writings departed from the conventional eighteenth-century theory of balanced government.

42. For an account of Montesquieu's combination of balanced government and the separation of powers, see Vile, *Constitutionalism*, chap. 4.

43. For an account of De Lolme's formative political experience in Geneva, see David Lieberman, introduction to Jean Louis De Lolme, *The Constitution of England; Or, An Account of the English Government*, ed. David Lieberman (Indianapolis: Liberty Fund, 2007), x–xii.

44. Ibid., 139, 143–44.

45. Ibid., 147.

46. Ibid., 145–46.

47. Ibid., 146.

48. Ibid., 147.

49. Among functions of the executive, it should be noted, De Lolme also lists the king's role in the legislative body and his role as the sole executive power.

50. De Lolme, *Constitution*, 261.

51. Ibid., 143–44.

52. Ibid., 139.

53. *Works*, 4: 371–73.

54. Ibid., 4: 371. Montesquieu had presented a version of the traditional maxim: "In a way, the nobility is of the essence of monarchy, whose fundamental maxim is: *no monarch, no nobility: no nobility, no monarch;* rather, one has a despot." See *Spirit of the Laws*, bk. 2, chap. 4.

55. Ibid., 4: 320.

56. Ibid., 4: 355. Adams's discussion of the contest of power between the king and the aristocracy resembles Hamilton's

account in *Federalist* 17 of the age-old contest between the sovereign and his subordinate vassals. Hamilton's point, however, was not to demonstrate the sovereign's role in controlling the vassals, but to compare the contest between sovereign and vassals with the "rivalship of power" that takes place in confederacies between the sovereign and the subordinate state authorities. See Hamilton, Madison, and Jay, *The Federalist*.

57. Ibid., 4: 585. For an account of Adams's executive as a defender of the people, see Palmer, *Age of the Democratic Revolution*, 273.

58. Adams to Jefferson, 9 July 1813, *The Adams-Jefferson Letters*.

59. Jefferson to Adams, 28 October 1813, ibid.

60. In this judgment I follow Joseph J. Ellis, who writes that Adams's ostracism scheme "was more a gimmick than an idea and more a measure of his desperation at finding an answer to what he regarded as the central dilemma of political science." See Ellis, *Passionate Sage*, 153.

61. Niccolò Machiavelli, *The Prince*, trans. Harvey C. Mansfield (Chicago: University of Chicago Press, 1998), 39. Ibid., bk. 1, chap. 3; ibid., chap. 9; and *Discourses on Livy*, trans. Harvey C. Mansfield and Nathan Tarcov (Chicago: University of Chicago Press, 1998), bk. 1, chaps. 3–5, 16. Of course, Machiavelli (and Machiavellianism) is often recalled in association with cynicism, cunning, and instrumental power politics, but as John McCormick has brought to light, Machiavelli was in fact a critic of socioeconomic elites and a shrewd analyst of the relation between class and political institutions. For an account of "class-specific" institutions in Machiavelli's writings, see McCormick, *Machiavellian Democracy*, chap. 4.

62. *Works*, 4: 559. For an extended account of Machiavelli's influence on Adams's *Defence*, see C. Bradley Thompson,

"John Adams's Machiavellian Moment," *Review of Politics* 57 (1995): 389–417.

63. Page Smith, *John Adams*, vol. 2, *1784–1826*, 701.

64. *Works*, 8: 448.

65. Ibid., 6: 10.

66. Ibid., 5: 11–105.

67. Niccolò Machiavelli, *History of Florence and the Affairs of Italy from the Earliest Time to the Death of Lorenzo the Magnificent* (New York: Harper & Row, 1960), 116.

68. *Works*, 5: 24.

69. Darren Staloff has traced Adams's preoccupation with the history of aristocracy to his engagement with the histories of feudalism found in the works of Edward Gibbon, William Robertson, and David Hume. See Staloff, "John Adams and the Enlightenment," in *A Companion to John Adams and John Quincy Adams*, ed. David Waldstreicher (Malden, MA: Wiley-Blackwell, 2013), 44–50.

70. *Works*, 6: 415.

71. Ibid., 4: 195. For accounts of the "mirror" or "likeness" notion of representation, see Storing, *What the Anti-Federalists Were For*, 17; Jack N. Rakove, *Original Meanings: Politics and Ideas in the Making of the Constitution* (New York: Vintage Books, 1996), chap. 8; and Bernard Manin, *The Principles of Representative Government* (Cambridge: Cambridge University Press, 1997), 109–12.

72. *Works*, 4: 381.

73. Ibid., 4: 552.

74. Ibid., 4: 410. Adams drew this observation directly from Machiavelli's *Discourses*. See Machiavelli, *Discourses on Livy*, bk. 1, chap. 3.

75. *Works*, 4: 523.

76. Ibid., 4: 355.

77. Ibid., 4: 296, 382.

78. Ibid., 4: 468.

79. Ibid., 4: 440.

80. Ibid., 4: 293.

81. Ibid., 4: 488.

82. Ibid., 4: 492.

83. Ibid., 4: 343–46.

84. Ibid., 4: 343–45. Some have traced Adams's view of aristo-cratic passions to an underlying Calvinist theology. John P. Diggins argued that the vanities and desires for distinc-tion that Adams attributed to aristocrats are best under-stood as varieties of the sin of pride. See Diggins, *The Lost Soul of American Politics*, 69–71. Thompson has cautioned against Diggins's view, arguing that Adams largely rejected Calvinism early in life and adopted an enlightenment-rationalist worldview—"a view of nature, man, and moral obligation that drew heavily on the enlightened views of Bacon, Newton, and Locke." Thompson, *John Adams and the Spirit of Liberty*, 5–6.

85. *Works*, 4: 444–45.

86. Ibid., 4: 354–57.

87. Ibid., 4: 362–65.

88. Ibid., 4: 363–66.

89. Ibid., 4: 366.

90. See Smith, *John Adams*, vol. 2, *1784–1826*, 774–76.

91. James Hillhouse, *Propositions for Amending the Constitution of the United States* (New Haven, CT: Oliver Steele, 1808).

92. *Works*, 6: 533.

93. Ibid., 4: 400.

94. Ibid., 4: 585. For an account of Adams's executive as a de-fender of the people, see Palmer, *Age of the Democratic Rev-olution*, 273. Oddly enough, Adams's antiaristocratic defense

of a powerful executive would be echoed in Anti-Federalist writings. A [Maryland] Farmer turned to a popular executive as a constitutional solution to the problem of aristocratic domination: "The only remedy the ingenuity of man has discovered for this evil is—a *properly constituted and independent executive*, a vindex injuriarum—an avenger of public wrongs; who with the assistance of a third estate, may enforce the rigor of equal law on those who are otherwise above the fear of punishment" (*The Complete Anti-Federalist*, 7 vols., ed. Herbert J. Storing [Chicago: University of Chicago Press, 1981], 5: 20).

95. Adams to Jefferson, 6 December 1787, *Adams-Jefferson Letters*, 213.

Chapter Two: The Goods of Fortune

1. John Adams, *Works*, 4: 392.

2. R. B. Bernstein, *Thomas Jefferson* (Oxford: Oxford University Press, 2003), 183; Joseph J. Ellis has described the correspondence as "the intellectual capstone to the achievements of the revolutionary generation." See Ellis, *American Sphinx: The Character of Thomas Jefferson* (New York: Vintage Books, 1998), xv.

3. Jefferson to Adams, 21 January 1812, *The Adams-Jefferson Letters*; Jefferson had, however, continued to keep abreast of political matters through regular contact with Madison, Monroe, and others. See McCullough, *John Adams*, 604.

4. For an account of the viciousness of the 1800 presidential election, see ibid., 536–47.

5. Abigail Adams to Thomas Jefferson, 1 July 1804, *Adams-Jefferson Letters*. "The serpent you cherished and warmed, bit the hand that nourished him, and gave you sufficient specimens of his talents, his gratitude, his justice, and his

truth. When such vipers are let loose upon society, all distinction between virtue and vice are leveled, all respect for character is lost." Abigail was referring here to Callender's allegation about Jefferson's sexual liaison with his slave Sally Hemings.

6. It is highly likely that Adams and Jefferson would have remained estranged from one another had it not been for the persistent efforts of Benjamin Rush, the renowned physician and fellow signer of the Declaration of Independence who had long been a dear friend and admirer of both men. Rush began his efforts to reunite them in the fall of 1809. In a letter to Adams, Rush recounted a dream, set in the future, that began with Rush's encounter with a page of the history of the United States. The page read that in November of 1809, a remarkable event occurred: "the renewal of the friendship and intercourse between Mr. John Adams and Mr. Jefferson, the two ex-Presidents of the United States." The renewed friendship took the form of a "correspondence of several years" and included reflections on past political engagements as well as "many precious aphorisms, the result of observation, experience, and profound reflection." The history book recounted that the two gentlemen, having left their letters to posterity, "sunk into the grave nearly at the same time, full of years and rich in the gratitude and praises of their country." Rush's appeal failed at first. Adams showed no interest in renewing the correspondence, and an appeal by Rush to Jefferson a year later was similarly rebuffed. Adams appreciated Rush's attempt. "I have no other objection to your dream," he wrote, "but that it is not history. It may be prophecy." In truth, the dream turned out to be more prophetic than Adams could have imagined. Beginning in 1812, after Rush finally succeeded in nudging Adams to reach out to his old

friend, the two ex-presidents carried on a correspondence that would continue until their final days. And not only did the two sink into the grave "nearly at the same time" as Rush had dreamed. They both died, famously, on July 4, 1826, exactly fifty years after the Declaration of Independence. See Benjamin Rush to John Adams, 16 October 1809, John A. Schutz and Douglass Adair, eds., *The Spur of Fame: Dialogues of John Adams and Benjamin Rush, 1805–1813* (San Marino, CA: Huntington Library: 1966); Adams to Rush, 25 October 1809, ibid.; Jefferson to Adams, 21 January 1812, *Adams-Jefferson Letters*.

7. Jefferson, *Writings*, 671.

8. Jefferson recalled that he had supported the Constitution along with amendments "favorable to freedom." Indeed, in a November 1787 letter to Jefferson, Adams had voiced his opinion that a "Declaration of Rights" should have preceded the Constitution's model of government. Adams to Jefferson, 10 November 1787, *Adams-Jefferson Letters*.

9. Jefferson to Adams, 27 June 1813, ibid.

10. Adams to Jefferson, 15 July 1813, ibid.

11. Jefferson to Adams, 28 October 1813, ibid. I discuss Jefferson's ideas about education and land reform later in this chapter.

12. Thomas Paine, *Rights of Man*, ed. Gregory Claeys (Indianapolis: Hackett, 1992), 73–74.

13. Ibid., 51.

14. Quoted in Andrew Jainchill, *Reimagining Politics after the Terror: The Republican Origins of French Liberalism* (Ithaca, NY: Cornell University Press, 2008), 129–36.

15. See Jonathan Elliot, ed., *The Debates in the Several State Conventions on the Adoption of the Federal Constitution, as Recommended by the General Convention at Philadelphia in*

1787, 5 vols. (Washington, DC: United States Congress, 1836), 2: 440–41.

16. Jefferson to Adams, 28 October 1813, *Adams-Jefferson Letters*.

17. James Madison, *Writings*, 165.

18. Ibid., 79.

19. Ibid., 81.

20. Jefferson to Adams, 28 October 1813, *Adams-Jefferson Letters*.

21. Jefferson to Lafayette, 16 June 1792, in Jefferson, *Writings*. For commentary on Bolingbroke's critique of Walpolean corruption, see Isaac Kramnick, *Bolingbroke and His Circle: The Politics of Nostalgia in the Age of Walpole* (Cambridge, MA: Harvard University Press, 1968). For analysis of the adaptation of anti-court ideology by the Jeffersonians, see Lance Banning, *The Jeffersonian Persuasion: Evolution of a Party Ideology* (Ithaca, NY: Cornell University Press, 1978).

22. Referring to Hamilton's efforts to use the levers of the Treasury to corrupt the legislature, Jefferson wrote: "Too many of these stock jobbers & king-jobbers have come into our legislature, or rather too many of our legislature have become stock jobbers & king-jobbers" (*Writings*, 990–91).

23. Madison, *Writings*, 509–11.

24. Ibid.

25. Jefferson to Adams, 28 October 1813, *Adams-Jefferson Letters*.

26. "A Bill for the More General Diffusion of Knowledge," Jefferson, *Writings*, 365–73.

27. Jefferson, *Writings*, 274.

28. Jefferson to Adams, 28 October 1813, *Adams-Jefferson Letters*.

29. Jefferson, *Writings*, 365.

30. James Harrington, *"The Commonwealth of Oceana" and "A System of Politics"* (Cambridge: Cambridge University Press, 1992), 23.

31. *Republic of Plato*, 415a–c.

32. Jefferson to Adams, 28 October 1813, *Adams-Jefferson Letters.*
33. Adams to Jefferson, 9 July 1813, ibid.
34. *Works*, 4: 397.
35. Ibid., 4: 392–97.
36. Ibid., 4: 395.
37. Adams to Jefferson, 9 July 1813, *Adams-Jefferson Letters.*
38. Adams to Jefferson, 15 September 1813, ibid.
39. Though Adams gave ample attention to a number of qualities as sources of influence, he wrote most frequently of wealth and birth. And between these two, wealth was paramount: "Fortune, it is true, has more influence than birth; a rich man of an ordinary family, and common decorum of conduct, may have greater weight than any family merit commonly confers without it" (*Works*, 4: 397).
40. Ibid., 4: 397.
41. Ibid., 4: 392.
42. Harrington, *"The Commonwealth of Oceana,"* 11.
43. *Works* 4: 397.
44. Ibid., 6: 501.
45. Ibid., 4: 392, 397.
46. Adams to Jefferson, 13 July 1813, *Adams-Jefferson Letters.*
47. Although Jefferson was long assumed by historians of American political thought to have been the American apostle of Rousseau's political philosophy, it was in fact Adams who probably read the Genevan's works more extensively and enthusiastically than any than any other American of the Founding Era. See Paul Merrill Spurlin, *Rousseau in America: 1760–1809* (Tuscaloosa, AL: University of Alabama Press, 1969). Adams owned a 1764, nine-volume edition of Rousseau's *Oeuvres* and recorded extensive marginalia on several of Rousseau's works. He had read Rousseau at least as early as 1765, when he studied *Of the Social Contract* in preparation for Jeremiah Gridley's young men's reading club, and he drew on

the work for a critique of feudal hierarchy in his *Dissertation on the Canon and Feudal Law*. Before the French Revolution drew wider attention to Rousseau's writings on both sides of the Atlantic, Adams is the only American recorded to have engaged with Rousseau's *Dissertation on Political Economy* and his *Considerations on Poland*. Rousseau seems to have provoked in Adams a mixture of admiration and indignation. Writing to his wife in 1778, Adams urged her to read Rousseau—a man "too virtuous for the Age." See John Adams to Abigail Adams, 2 December 1778, *The Adams Papers*, vol. 3. Yet Adams was more often critical. Rousseau's concept of the general will was "too mathematical or too witty to be very clear," and the idea of self-government sketched in *Dissertation on Political Economy* prompted Adams to exclaim, "It is amazing that eyes so piercing should be so blind." See Haraszti, *John Adams and the Prophets of Progress*, 95.

48. Haraszti, *John Adams and the Prophets of Progress*, 89, 88, 88 (my emphasis), 89, 91.
49. Ibid., 87.
50. *Works*, 4: 392.
51. Ibid., 5: 457.
52. Ibid., 4: 398.
53. Ibid., 15.
54. Ibid., 23.
55. Ibid., 24. Caroline Robbins has influentially traced a tradition of republican ideology stretching from mid-seventeenth-century figures such as Harrington, Marchamont Nedham, and Algernon Sidney to the writings of revolutionary America. See Robbins, *The Eighteenth-Century Commonwealthman: Studies in the Transmission, Development, and Circumstance of English Liberal Thought from the Restoration of Charles II Until the War with the Thirteen Colonies* (Indianapolis: Liberty Fund, 2004).

56. Adams to Jefferson, 15 September 1813, *Adams Jefferson Letters*.

57. John Taylor, *An Inquiry into the Principles and Policy of the Government of the United States* (New Haven, CT, 1814), 34. For a sympathetic interpretation of Taylor's critique, see Wood, *The Creation of the American Republic*, 588–92.

58. Taylor, *Inquiry*, 51, 36.

59. Ibid., 46–47.

60. Ibid., 81, 46–47.

61. *Works*, 6: 461. Joseph J. Ellis, who has written the most insightful account available of the Adams-Taylor exchange, interprets Adams as insinuating that pronouncements on social equality carried no credibility when uttered by the likes of Taylor, a slave-owning patrician. See Ellis, *Passionate Sage*, 143–60.

62. Adams to Jefferson, 15 September 1813, *Adams-Jefferson Letters*; *Works*, 9: 638; Adams to Rush, 27 December 1810, Schutz and Adair, *Spur of Fame*. The national bank that Adams prescribed would have a branch in each state. For a careful treatment of the difference between Adams and Taylor on the issue of the banking system, see Ellis, *Passionate Sage*, 162–65. Ellis writes that Adams "harbored a deep-seated distrust of banks as sanctuaries for corrupt profiteers, gambling houses where the public trust was systematically put at risk and sold to the highest bidder." And yet Adams did not share Taylor's proto-Jacksonian view of banks as "conspiratorial agencies operating in collusion with government to defy and distort the natural laws of the marketplace."

63. *Works*, 6: 531.

64. Ibid., 6: 454–56, 6: 456–58, 6: 454–56.

65. Ibid., 6: 451.

66. Ibid., 6: 456–57. Though I contend that Adams was not an "aristocrat" in the sense of being committed to aristocratic

privilege, it should be noted that Adams was indeed an aristocrat according to his own definition.

67. Joseph Ellis notes that Adams "had a maddening tendency to expand and contract his definition of aristocracy without warning." See Ellis, *Passionate Sage*, 159.

68. *Works*, 6: 457.

69. Ibid., 6: 500–501.

70. Ibid., 6: 504–6.

71. Adams to Jefferson, 9 July 1813 and 16 August 1813, *Adams-Jefferson Letters*. It should be noted that Adams did not altogether reject the ideal of a natural aristocracy of merit. As we have seen in chapter 1, he held out the possibility that the very same men who were most threatening could be of great benefit to republics if their energies were properly checked and channeled. In this respect, Adams followed Bolingbroke, who had described an extraordinary class of men whose effect on the political community could be good or bad, but never neutral. In a passage quoted by Adams, Bolingbroke announced that such men could be "the guardian angels of the country . . . studious to avert the most distant evil, and to procure peace, plenty, and the greatest of human blessings, liberty." However, Bolingbroke warned, the very same men could also appear in public life as "the instruments of Divine vengeance," leaving behind them a path "marked by desolation and oppression, by poverty and servitude" (*Works*, 4: 413–14).

72. Ibid., 4: 400–401.

73. David Hume, *Essays: Moral, Political, and Literary*, ed. Eugene F. Miller (Indianapolis: Liberty Fund, 1985), 512–29.

74. A selection scheme similar to Hume's is found in Madison's design for the Senate in the so-called Virginia Plan, his rough blueprint for a new constitution that served as the subject of the opening deliberations of the Federal Convention.

See Max Farrand, ed., *Records of the Federal Convention of 1787*, vol. 1 (New Haven, CT: Yale University Press, 1966), 15–28 and 50–51; and Daniel Wirls and Stephen Wirls, *The Invention of the United States Senate* (Baltimore: Johns Hopkins University Press, 2004), 66–67.

75. *Works*, 4: 466–68.

76. Ibid., 4: 517.

77. Ibid., 6: 519.

78. Adams to Jefferson, 2 September 1813, *Adams-Jefferson Letters*.

79. *Works*, 4: 556–57.

80. Ibid., 6: 494–95.

81. Ibid., 6: 519.

82. Madame Bowdoin was niece of the wealthy former Massachusetts governor and proprietor James Bowdoin II, and had been the wife of James Bowdoin III.

83. Adams to Jefferson, 19 December 1813, *Adams-Jefferson Letters*.

84. Adams to Jefferson, 2 September 1813, ibid.

85. Adams to Jefferson, 15 November 1813, ibid.

86. Adams to Jefferson, 16 August 1813, ibid.

CHAPTER THREE: SYMPATHY FOR THE RICH

1. Alexis de Tocqueville, *Democracy in America*, ed. Harvey C. Mansfield and Delba Winthrop (Chicago: University of Chicago Press, 2000), 171, 50. Tocqueville suggested that aristocratic power relied on landed wealth, transferred hereditarily from one generation to the next. Aristocracy "takes to the land; it attaches to the soil and leans on it; it is not established by privileges alone, nor constituted by birth." It was no wonder, then, that even when something resembling aristocracy appeared in America, it was "a sort of aristocracy

little different from the mass of the people, whose passions and interests it easily embraced, exciting neither love nor hate." Rather than "sustain an often unequal struggle against the poorest of their fellow citizens," the rich in America preferred to abandon political life. "Not being able to take up a rank in public life analogous to the one they occupy in private life, they abandon the first to concentrate on the second." Even as the rich man publicly extols the advantages of democratic forms, he in fact "submits to this state of things as to an irremediable evil." The rich man's frustration was evident in the disparity between his public modesty on the one hand and his private indulgence in luxury on the other. Ibid, 30, 46, 171.

2. Robert Dahl, *Who Governs? Democracy and Power in an American City* (New Haven, CT: Yale University Press, 2005), 85. For other versions of the pluralist theory, which long dominated the field of political science, see V. O. Key Jr., *Politics, Parties, and Pressure Groups*, 5th ed. (New York: Crowell, 1964); David B. Truman, *The Governmental Process: Political Interests and Public Opinion* (New York: Knopf, 1951).

3. G. William Domhoff, *Who Rules America?* chap. 4.

4. See Hacker and Pierson, *Winner-Take-All Politics* and Schlozman, Verba, and Brady, *Unheavenly Chorus*.

5. See Winters, *Oligarchy*, chap. 5.

6. *Works*, 4: 444–45. A portion of every electorate, wrote Adams, would be "profligate and unprincipled" and therefore vulnerable to "entertainments, secret intrigues, and every popular art, and even to bribes" (ibid., 4: 444). Riches, moreover, could purchase more subtle political advantages. The wealthy could buy the type of education that would cultivate superior abilities, they could afford to groom their appearance for popular appeal, and they could afford to endow

their family names with prestige by erecting costly monuments (ibid., 6: 235). As discussed in chapter 2, the ability of the rich to buy influence was heightened by the relations of material dependency that accompanied conditions of inequality.

7. *The Republic of Plato*, 544d5–555b1.

8. My emphasis. David Hume, *Essays Moral, Political, and Literary*, ed. T. H. Green and T. H. Grose (London: Longmans, Green, 1875), 1: 109; my emphasis.

9. *Works*, 6: 482.

10. Lovejoy, *Reflections on Human Nature*, 201.

11. Adams remarked that "president" was a title given to heads of fire companies and cricket clubs.

12. For an overview of the Senate's debate over presidential titles, see Stanley Elkins and Eric McKitrick, *The Age of Federalism: The Early American Republic, 1788–1800* (New York: Oxford University Press, 1993), 46–48. I discuss this episode in chapter 4.

13. *Works*, 9: 563. Adams also worried about the anticlerical agenda of the revolutionaries: "I know not what to make of a republic of thirty million atheists." Quoted in McCullough, *John Adams*, 418.

14. Lovejoy, *Reflections on Human Nature*, 34.

15. *Works*, 3: 432–37.

16. Mills, *The Power Elite*, 89–93.

17. For discussion of the influence of Scottish Enlightenment moral psychology on Adams's evolving view of human nature, see Staloff, "John Adams and the Enlightenment," 50–52.

18. For an analysis and critique of the evocation of sympathy in Harriet Beecher Stowe's *Uncle Tom's Cabin*, see Marianne Noble, *The Masochistic Pleasures of Sentimental Literature* (Princeton, NJ: Princeton University Press, 2000), chap. 4.

19. John Millar, *An Historical View of the English Government from the Settlement of the Saxons in Britain, to the Revolution in 1688* (London, 1818), 287–90.

20. Adam Ferguson, *An Essay on the History of Civil Society*, 3rd edition (London, 1768), 420–23.

21. Millar, *Historical View*, 288–89. For an extended discussion of the themes of rank and authority in the social thought of the Scottish Enlightenment, see Christopher J. Berry, *Social Theory of the Scottish Enlightenment* (Edinburgh: Edinburgh University Press, 1997), 99–104.

22. Adam Smith, *The Theory of Moral Sentiments*, 43, 43–51.

23. Ibid., 46–47.

24. Ibid., 50–53.

25. Ibid., 61–63, 52.

26. Ibid., 52, 50–51. Writing of kings, Smith noted that only the misfortunes of lovers provoked a comparable sympathy.

27. *Works*, 6: 232–34.

28. See Martin Luther King, Jr., "The Drum Major Instinct (4 February 1968)," in *A Testament of Hope: The Essential Writings and Speeches of Martin Luther King, Jr.* (New York: HarperOne, 2003), 259–67. King followed Adams both by identifying the desire for distinction as the predominant human motive and by calling for that desire to be harnessed for the good of the public. In his "Drum Major Instinct" sermon, King preached that the instinct, though dangerous, should be harnessed and channeled toward righteous ends. For comparison of Adams and King, see Bruce Miroff, *Icons of Democracy: American Leaders as Heroes, Aristocrats, Dissenters, and Democrats* (Lawrence: University Press of Kansas, 2000), chap. 9.

29. *Works*, 6: 245.

30. For a discussion of Adams's take on the republican uses of the passion for distinction, see Bruce Miroff, "Merit, Fame, and Political Leadership," 116–32.

31. *Works*, 6: 248.
32. Ibid., 6: 242.
33. Ibid., 6: 236.
34. Several passages in Adams's discussion are mere paraphrases of Smith's words. However, it should be noted that Adams engaged with Smith's text creatively. As Zoltán Haraszti has pointed out, Adams's phrasing "is often more powerful than Smith's" and "his passion for stringing together epithets and metaphors makes his presentation particularly vivid." See Haraszti, *John Adams and the Prophets of Progress*, 169.
35. *Works*, 6: 237.
36. Ibid., 6: 238.
37. Ibid., 6: 95. Adams's description of emulation anticipated the later work of Thorsten Veblen, who famously argued in his *Theory of the Leisure Class* that wealth was coveted not just for its pleasure-maximizing function but as a source of social distinction. For a discussion of the antecedents of Veblen's theory in eighteenth-century social thought, see Lovejoy, *Reflections on Human Nature*, 208–15.
38. *Works*, 6: 239.
39. Albert O. Hirschman, *The Passions and the Interests: Political Arguments for Capitalism Before its Triumph* (Princeton, NJ: Princeton University Press, 1997), 63–66. My account of the late-eighteenth-century distinction between the "passions" and the "interests" is drawn entirely from Hirschman's work.
40. Quoted in Hirschman, *The Passions and the Interests*, 58.
41. *Works*, 4: 407.
42. Ibid., 6: 238.
43. Tocqueville, *Democracy in America*, 599.
44. Ibid., 530–32.
45. Ibid., 601.
46. *Works*, 4: 95.

47. Ibid., 6: 263. In addition to bestowing influence on wealth, Adams observed, the widespread sympathy for the rich tended to set off contests among the politically ambitious to outdo one another in displays of luxury: "A universal emulation in luxury instantly commences; and the governors, that is, those who aspire at elections, are obliged to take the lead in this silly contention; they must not be behind the foremost in dress, equipage, furniture, entertainments, games, races, spectacles; they must feast and gratify the luxury of electors to obtain their votes." The end result was the commercialization of the offices of government, as "the whole executive authority must be prostituted, and the legislative too, to encourage luxury" (ibid, 6: 97).

48. Adams to Jefferson, 2 September 1813, *Adams-Jefferson Letters*. Adams insisted that beauty had prevailed over competing qualities even in the minds of "men of the highest rank, greatest power, and, sometimes, the most exalted genius, greatest fame, and highest merit."

49. Ibid., 6: 452–54.

50. Ibid., 6: 235.

51. Ibid., 4: 392.

52. David Brooks, "The Triumph of Hope over Self-Interest," *New York Times*, 12 January 2003.

53. Smith quoted in *Works*, 6: 258.

54. Tocqueville, *Democracy in America*, 171.

55. I will return to this point in the conclusion.

56. Adams to Jefferson, 9 October 1787, *Adams-Jefferson Letters*.

57. Adams to Rush, 28 July 1789, in Adams, *Old Family Letters: Copied from the Originals for Alexander Biddle* (Philadelphia: J. B. Lippincott, 1892).

58. Haraszti, *John Adams and the Prophets of Progress*, 202–3.

59. *Works*, 6: 95.

60. Tocqueville, *Democracy in America*, 594.

61. *Works*, 6: 271.
62. *Works*, 4: 395; Edmund Burke, *Reflections on the Revolution in France*, ed. J.G.A. Pocock (Indianapolis: Hackett, 1987), 169.
63. Huntington, *American Politics*, 38.
64. Nye *Soft Power*, x.

CHAPTER FOUR: DIGNIFIED DEMOCRACY

1. William Maclay, *Journal of William Maclay*, ed. Edgar S. Maclay (New York: D. Appleton and Company, 1890), 10, 22.
2. *Works*, 6: 243.
3. Maclay, *Journal of William Maclay*, 10–11.
4. Ibid., 2–3.
5. Ibid., 11–13.
6. Smith, *John Adams, 1784–1826*, 2:758.
7. For an account of the rise of the Democratic-Republican movement in the early 1790s, see Wilentz, *The Rise of American Democracy*, chap. 2.
8. See Elkins and McKitrick, *The Age of Federalism*, 237–39.
9. *National Intelligencer* (Washington: 6 March 1801). For a description of Adams's inaugural ceremony, see Page Smith, *John Adams*, 2: 917. For a comparison of Adams's inaugural with Jefferson's first inaugural, see John Ferling, *Jefferson and Hamilton: The Rivalry that Forged a Nation* (New York: Bloomsbury, 2013), 333.
10. *Works*, 6: 395.
11. See chapter 2.
12. *Works*, 6: 241.
13. Adams to Jefferson, 29 July 1791, *Adams-Jefferson Letters*.
14. Letter to Mercy Otis Warren, 8 August 1807, Founders Online, National Archives (http://founders.archives.gov/documents/Adams/99–02–02–5203 [last update 2015–12–30]).

15. See chapter 1.

16. Adams to Benjamin Rush, 28 July 1789, in Adams, *Old Family Letters*. It should be noted that Adams also hoped that titles would subordinate state governments to the new federal government. See Adams to William Tudor, 9 May 1789, Founders Online, National Archives (http://founders .archives.gov/documents/Adams/99–02–02–0550 [last update 2015–12–30]). For a discussion of the role of titles in assuring appropriate relations of subordination, see John R. Howe Jr., *The Changing Political Thought of John Adams* (Princeton, NJ: Princeton University Press, 1966), 178–79.

17. Adams to Rush, 28 July, 1789, *Old Family Letters*.

18. Sallust, *The War with Catiline*, trans. J. C. Rolfe, Loeb Classical Library (Cambridge, MA: Harvard University Press, 1921), 7.6. John Adams referred to Sallust as "one of the most polished and perfect of the Roman historians." See John Adams to John Quincy Adams, 18 May 1781, *The Adams Papers*, vol. 4. David Grewal has observed that Sallust's view of the public benefits yielded by the competition for glory anticipates the early-modern economic theory that derives public benefits from self-interested individual activity. See Grewal, "The Political Theology of Laissez Faire: From *Philia* to Self-Love in Commercial Society." *Political Theology* 17 (forthcoming).

19. Saint Augustine, *Concerning the City of God against the Pagans*, trans. Henry Bettenson (New York: Penguin, 2003), chaps. 12 and 13.

20. See Montesquieu, *The Spirit of the Laws*, bk. 2, chap. 4; bk. 3, chaps. 6–10; bk. 5, chaps. 11, 12, and 14. For an extended discussion of Montesquieu's view of the role of honor in monarchies, and for a thematic discussion of the role of honor in dividing and controlling power, see Sharon Krause, *Liberalism with Honor* (Cambridge, MA: Harvard University Press,

2002). For commentary on David Hume's account of how a similar system of honor was institutionalized in England under Edward III, see Andrew Sabl, *Hume's Politics: Coordination and Crisis in the History of England* (Princeton, NJ: Princeton University Press, 2012), 69–70.

21. There were also some who held the opposite view. For many students of Montesquieu in Founding Era America, it was assumed that public-spirited virtue, rather than honor or the desire for public distinction, should be the animating force of the American political system. America, after all, was a republic, or at least a federation of republics, not a monarchy. Montesquieu had stated clearly that republics relied on virtue alone. See Dumas Malone's discussion of the lessons Thomas Jefferson took from Montesquieu, in *Jefferson the Virginian* (Charlottesville: University of Virginia Press, 2006), 176–79. See also Herbert Storing's discussion of Anti-Federalist theories of civic virtue and the small republic, in *What the Anti-Federalists Were For*, 19–21.

22. Hamilton criticized the idea of a term-limited chief executive on the grounds that no man seeking fame would undertake arduous enterprises for the public benefit if he could foresee that "he must quit the scene before he could accomplish the work, and must commit that, together with his own reputation, to hands which might be unequal or unfriendly to the task" (Alexander Hamilton, James Madison, and John Jay, *The Federalist*, ed. T. Ball [Cambridge: Cambridge University Press, 2003], no. 71. For an influential account of the desire for fame as a leading motivation of Founding Era American statesmen, see Douglass Adair, *Fame and the Founding Fathers*, ed. Trevor Colbourn (New York: W. W. Norton & Company, 1972), 14–19. For commentary on Hamilton's theory of the love of fame and the relevance of that theory for contemporary democratic politics, see Andrew Sabl, *Ruling Passions: Political Offices and Democratic Ethics* (Princeton, NJ:

Princeton University Press, 2002), 77–84, 164–66, 271. For a survey of accounts of the love of fame in the broader history of political thought, and for a sympathetic critique of this motive from the perspective of David Hume's writings, see Sabl, "Noble Infirmity: Love of Fame in Hume," *Political Theory* 34 (October 2006), 542–68.

23. Hamilton, Madison, and Jay, *Federalist*, no. 51.

24. *Works*, 6: 209.

25. Ibid., 6: 241.

26. Ibid., 6: 243. For an extended discussion of Adams's intention to use the "language of signs" both to spur men to seek noble ands and also to foster obedience and attachment to laws, see Thompson, *John Adams and the Spirit of Liberty*, 222–27. The most comprehensive account of Adams's effort to promote public-spirited activity through the use of titles is found in Miroff, *Icons of Democracy*, chap. 2.

27. *Works*, 271.

28. Burke, *Reflections*, 33, 169.

29. See Judith N. Shklar, *Ordinary Vices* (Cambridge, MA: Belknap Press of Harvard University Press, 1984), 90–101.

30. *Works*, 4: 395.

31. As discussed in chapter 2, Adams probably read Rousseau's works more extensively and carefully than any other American of the Founding Era.

32. Jean-Jacques Rousseau, *Considerations on the Government of Poland and on its Projected Reformation* in *Rousseau: The Social Contract and Other Political Writings*, ed. and trans. by Victor Gourevitch (Cambridge: Cambridge University Press, 1997).

33. Here Adams was likely referring to the Society of the Cincinnati, which had attempted to establish hereditary military honors in post-Revolution America. Years earlier, Adams had denounced the Society of the Cincinnati as, among other things, "an effectual subversion of our equality." See

Adams to Elbridge Gerry, 25 April 1785, Gilder Lehrman Institute of American History, Gilder Lehrman Collection no. GLC00366 (http://www.gilderlehrman.org/collections /eb84c4fb-1e3e-4198–816c-556348921328).

34. Adams to Rush, 20 June 1808, in Schutz and Adair, *Spur of Fame.*

35. Thomas Paine, *Collected Writings* (New York: Library of America, 1995), 462–78.

36. Maclay, *Journal of William Maclay,* 23.

37. Ibid. In using the word "philosophers," Maclay was deliberately twisting Adams's derisive use of the term during the debates, when Adams, after conceding that "philosophers" had found no use for titles, also pointed out that they had found no use for government.

38. Adams, notes on Mary Wollstonecraft's *Historical and Moral View of the Origin and Progress of the French Revolution,* in Zoltán Haraszti, *John Adams and the Prophets of Progress,* 188.

39. Writing of the most highly regarded stock-car racer in North Carolina, Wolfe explains: "Junior Johnson is one of the last of those sports stars who is not just an ace at the game itself, but a hero a whole people or class of people can identify with." See Wolfe, "The Last American Hero is Junior Johnson. Yes!" *Esquire* (March 1965), 71–74, 138–55.

40. In an unpublished study of wealth distribution in the early republic, Frank Garmon finds that inequality increased considerably through the year 1815, especially from 1805 to 1815. Garmon concluded that "the enormous disparities of wealth ownership suggest that Jefferson's visions of an egalitarian country composed of independent smallholders may have been incongruent with the realities of the Early Republic, and that recent trends in the American wealth holding may not be unprecedented." Frank W. Garmon Jr., "Wealth Levels and Distribution in the Early American Republic, 1785–1815," paper presented at the annual meeting

of the Economic History Association, Columbus, OH, 12–14 September 2014.

41. Ralph Waldo Emerson, *Essays and Lectures* (New York: Library of America, 1983), 262.

42. For a discussion of the difference between the premodern concept of honor and the modern idea of dignity that replaced it, see Peter Berger, "On the Obsolescence of the Concept of Honor," in *Revisions: Changing Perspectives in Moral Philosophy* (Notre Dame, IN: Notre Dame University Press, 1983).

43. Inti Laundaro, "French Economist Thomas Piketty Refuses Legion of Honor," *Wall Street Journal*, 1 January 2015 (http://www.wsj.com/articles/french-economist-thomas -piketty-refuses-legion-of-honor-1420).

44. For a discussion of Adams's view of the relationship between oligarchic passions and oligarchic power, see chapter 3.

CONCLUSION: AMERICAN OLIGARCHY?

1. Howe, *The Changing Political Thought of John Adams* xv; Schutz and Adair, "The Love of Fame, The Ruling Passion of the Noblest Minds," in *The Spur of Fame*, 18–19.

2. Quoted in Wood, *The Creation of the American Republic*, See John Stevens, *Observations on Government*.

3. Quoted in Wood, *Creation of the American Republic*, 587.

4. *Records of the Federal Convention of 1787*, vol. 1, 397–403.

5. Alexis De Tocqueville, *Democracy in America*, 35.

6. According to Tocqueville, the Revolution had swept away the last remnants of aristocracy in America. The abolition of primogeniture and the ensuing partition of land had eliminated the territorial basis of aristocracy, thereby destroying hereditary distinction and transforming the sons of "the great landed property owners" into "men of commerce, attorneys, doctors" and throwing many "into the most profound

obscurity." And even before the Revolution, the socioreligious background of the colonists and the American landscape had precluded the development of an aristocratic class. This was especially true of the New England colonies. But even west of the Hudson, where land was settled by rich men intending to establish aristocracy, the landscape resisted their attempts. Difficult as it was "to clear that rebellious land," the profit to be had was not sufficient "to enrich a master and a tenant at once." It was therefore necessary to divide the land into small estates, each cultivated by the property owner alone. Ibid., 30, 35, 46–50.

7. Louis Hartz, *The Liberal Tradition in America: An Interpretation of American Political Thought since the Revolution* (New York, Harcourt Books, 1991), 51.

8. Niebuhr thought that Jeffersonian liberalism was guilty of the same "pretensions of innocency" that characterized Soviet communism, whose "priest-kings" viewed themselves as innocent of evil even as they "gathered both economic and political control in the hands of a single oligarchy." See Reinhold Niebuhr, *The Irony of American History* (Chicago: University of Chicago Press, 2008), 20–23, 30–35.

9. *Works*, 4: 393.

10. Tocqueville, *Democracy in America*, 599.

11. Ibid., 488. Judith N. Shklar, *Ordinary Vices*, 90.

12. Tocqueville, *Democracy in America*, 553.

13. Thomas Piketty, *Capital in the Twenty-First Century* (Cambridge, MA: Harvard University Press, 2014), 265.

14. Charles Murray, *Coming Apart: The State of White America, 1960–2010* (New York: Crown Forum, 2012), 104–5.

15. *Works*, 4: 401.

Bibliography

Adair, Douglass. *Fame and the Founding Fathers*. Edited by Trevor Colbourn. New York: Norton, 1972.

Adams, John. Founders Online, National Archives (http://founders.archives.gov/about/Adams).

———. *The Adams-Jefferson Letters: The Complete Correspondence between Thomas Jefferson and Abigail and John Adams*. Edited by Lester J. Cappon (Chapel Hill: University of North Carolina Press, 1987).

———. *The Adams Papers: Adams Family Correspondence*. Vols. 3–4, *April 1778–September 1782*. Edited by L. H. Butterfield and Marc Friedlander. Cambridge, MA: Belknap Press of Harvard University Press, 1973.

———. *The Adams Papers: Adams Family Correspondence*. Vol. 8, *March 1787–December 1789*. Edited by Margaret A. Hogan, C. James Taylor, Hobson Woodward, Jessie May Rodrique, Gregg L. Lint, and Mary T. Claffey. Cambridge, MA: Belknap Press of Harvard University Press, 2007.

———. *Old Family Letters: Copied from the Originals for Alexander Biddle*. Philadelphia: J. B. Lippincott, 1892.

———. *The Works of John Adams, Second President of the United States*. 10 vols. Edited by Charles Francis Adams. Boston: Little, Brown, 1850–56.

Allen, Danielle. *Our Declaration: A Reading of the Declaration of Independence in Defense of Equality*. New York: W. W. Norton & Company, 2014.

Appleby, Joyce. *Liberalism and Republicanism in the Historical Imagination*. Cambridge, MA: Harvard University Press, 1992.

Arendt, Hannah. *On Revolution*. New York: Viking, 1963.

Aristotle. *Politics and the Constitution of Athens*. Edited by Stephen Everson. Cambridge: Cambridge University Press, 1996.

Augustine. *Concerning the City of God against the Pagans*. Translated by Henry Bettenson. New York: Penguin, 2003.

Banning, Lance. *The Jeffersonian Persuasion: Evolution of a Party Ideology*. Ithaca, NY: Cornell University Press, 1978.

Bartels, Larry M. *Unequal Democracy: The Political Economy of the New Gilded Age*. Princeton, NJ: Princeton University Press, 2008.

Bellamy, Richard. "The Political Form of the Constitution: The Separation of Powers, Rights, and Representative Democracy." *Political Studies* 44 (1996): 436–56.

Berger, Peter. "On the Obsolescence of the Concept of Honor." In *Revisions: Changing Perspectives in Moral Philosophy*, edited by Stanley Hauerwas and Alasdair MacIntyre, 172–81. Notre Dame, IN: Notre Dame University Press, 1983.

Bernstein, R. B. *Thomas Jefferson*. Oxford: Oxford University Press, 2003.

Berry, Christopher J. *Social Theory of the Scottish Enlightenment*. Edinburgh: Edinburgh University Press, 1997.

Burke, Edmund. *Reflections on the Revolution in France*. Edited by J.G.A. Pocock. Indianapolis: Hackett, 1987.

Dahl, Robert. *Who Governs? Democracy and Power in an American City*. New Haven, CT: Yale University Press, 2005.

De Lolme, Jean Louis. *The Constitution of England; Or, An Account of the English Government*. Edited by David Lieberman. Indianapolis: Liberty Fund, 2007.

Diamond, Martin. "Democracy and the Federalist: A Reconstruction of the Framers' Intent." *American Political Science Review* 53, no. 1 (1959): 52–68.

Diggins, John Patrick. *John Adams*. New York: Times Books, 2003.

———. *The Lost Soul of American Politics: Virtue, Self-Interest, and the Foundations of Liberalism*. Chicago: University of Chicago Press, 1984.

Domhoff, G. William. *Who Rules America? Power and Politics*. 4th ed. Boston: McGraw Hill, 2002.

Elkins, Stanley, and Eric McKitrick. *The Age of Federalism: The Early American Republic, 1788–1800*. New York: Oxford University Press, 1993.

Elliot, Jonathan, ed. *The Debates in the Several State Conventions on the Adoption of the Federal Constitution, as Recommended by the General Convention at Philadelphia in 1787*. 5 vols. Washington: United States Congress, 1836.

Ellis, Joseph J. *American Sphinx: The Character of Thomas Jefferson*. New York: Vintage Books, 1998.

———. *Passionate Sage: The Character and Legacy of John Adams*. New York: W.W. Norton & Company, 2001.

Elliot, Jonathan, ed., *The Debates in the Several State Conventions on the Adoption of the Federal Constitution, as Recommended by the General Convention at Philadelphia in 1787*, 5 vols. Washington, DC: United States Congress, 1836.

Emerson, Ralph Waldo. *Essays and Lectures*. New York: Library of America, 1983.

Farrand, Max. *The Framing of the Constitution*. New Haven, CT: Yale University Press, 1913.

———, ed. *Records of the Federal Convention of 1787*. Vol. 1. New Haven, CT: Yale University Press, 1966.

Ferguson, Adam. *An Essay on the History of Civil Society*. 3rd ed. London, 1768.

Ferling, John. *Jefferson and Hamilton: The Rivalry That Forged a Nation*. New York: Bloomsbury, 2013.

———. *John Adams: A Life*. Oxford: Oxford University Press, 1992.

Garmon, Frank W., Jr. "Wealth Levels and Distribution in the Early American Republic, 1785–1815." A paper presented at the annual meeting of the Economic History Association, Columbus, OH, 12–14 September 2014.

Gilens, Martin. *Affluence and Influence.* Princeton, NJ: Princeton University Press, 2012.

Grewal, David. "The Political Theology of Laissez Faire: From *Philia* to Self-Love in Commercial Society." *Political Theology* 17 (forthcoming).

Hacker, Jacob S., and Paul Pierson. *Winner-Take-All Politics: How Washington Made the Rich Richer—and Turned Its Back on the Middle Class.* New York: Simon & Schuster, 2010.

Hamilton, Alexander. *The Papers of Alexander Hamilton.* Vol. 5. Edited by Harold C. Syrett and Jacob E. Cooke. New York: Columbia University Press, 1962.

Hamilton, Alexander, James Madison, and John Jay. *The Federalist.* Edited by T. Ball. Cambridge: Cambridge University Press, 2003.

Handlin, Oscar, and Mary Flug Handlin. *Commonwealth: A Study of the Role of Government in the American Economy: Massachusetts, 1774–1861.* Cambridge, MA: Belknap Press of Harvard University Press.

Haraszti, Zoltán. *John Adams and the Prophets of Progress.* Cambridge, MA: Harvard University Press, 1952.

Harrington, James. *"The Commonwealth of Oceana" and "A System of Politics."* Cambridge: Cambridge University Press, 1992.

Hartz, Louis. *The Liberal Tradition in America: An Interpretation of American Political Thought since the Revolution.* New York: Harcourt Books, 1991.

Hillhouse, James. *Propositions for Amending the Constitution of the United States.* New Haven. CT: Oliver Steele, 1808.

Hirschman, Albert O. *The Passions and the Interests: Political*

Arguments for Capitalism before Its Triumph. Princeton, NJ: Princeton University Press, 1997.

Hobbes, Thomas. *Leviathan*. Edited by Richard Tuck. Cambridge: Cambridge University Press, 1996.

Hoekstra, Kinch. "Early Modern Absolutism and Constitutionalism." *Cardozo Law Review* 34 (2012–2013): 1079–98.

Homans, George C. "John Adams and the Constitution of Massachusetts." *Proceedings of the American Philosophical Society* 125, no. 4 (1981): 28–91.

Howe, John R., Jr. *The Changing Political Thought of John Adams*. Princeton, NJ: Princeton University Press, 1966.

Hume, David. *Essays Moral, Political, and Literary*. Edited by T. H. Green and T. H. Grose. London: Longmans, Green, 1875.

———. *Essays: Moral, Political, and Literary*. Edited by Eugene F. Miller. Indianapolis: Liberty Fund, 1985.

Huntington, Samuel P. *American Politics: The Promise of Disharmony*. Cambridge, MA: Harvard University Press, 1981.

Jainchill, Andrew. *Reimagining Politics after the Terror: The Republican Origins of French Liberalism*. Ithaca, NY: Cornell University Press, 2008.

Jefferson, Thomas. *The Papers of Thomas Jefferson*. Vol. 2, *January 1777 to June 1779*. Edited by Julian P. Boyd. Princeton, NJ: Princeton University Press, 1950.

———. *The Papers of Thomas Jefferson*. Vol. 11, *January 1787 to August 1787*. Edited by Julian P. Boyd. Princeton, NJ: Princeton University Press, 1959.

———. *Writings*. Edited by Merrill Peterson. New York: Library of America, 1984.

Journal of Debates and Proceedings in the Convention of Delegates Chosen to Revise the Constitution of Massachusetts. Boston: Office of the Daily Advertiser, 1821.

Key, V. O., Jr. *Politics, Parties, and Pressure Groups*. 5th ed. New York: Crowell, 1964.

King, Martin Luther, Jr. "The Drum Major Instinct (4 February 1968)." *A Testament of Hope: The Essential Writings and Speeches of Martin Luther King, Jr.* New York: HarperOne, 2003.

Kirk, Russell. *The Conservative Mind: From Burke to Eliot.* 7th rev. ed. Washington, DC: Regnery Publishing, 1985.

Kramnick, Isaac. *Bolingbroke and His Circle: The Politics of Nostalgia in the Age of Walpole.* Cambridge, MA: Harvard University Press, 1968.

Krause, Sharon. *Liberalism with Honor.* Cambridge, MA: Harvard University Press, 2002.

Lovejoy, Arthur O. *Reflections on Human Nature.* Baltimore: Johns Hopkins Press, 1961.

Machiavelli, Niccolò. *Discourses on Livy.* Translated by Harvey C. Mansfield and Nathan Tarcov. Chicago: University of Chicago Press, 1998.

———. *History of Florence and the Affairs of Italy from the Earliest Time to the Death of Lorenzo the Magnificent.* New York: Harper & Row, 1960.

———. *The Prince.* Translated by Harvey C. Mansfield. Chicago: University of Chicago Press, 1998.

Maclay, William. *Journal of William Maclay.* Edited by Edgar S. Maclay. New York: D. Appleton, 1890.

Madison, James. *Writings.* Edited by Jack N. Rakove. New York: Library of America, 1999.

Malone, Dumas. *Jefferson the Virginian.* Charlottesville: University of Virginia Press, 2006.

Manin, Bernard. *The Principles of Representative Government.* Cambridge: Cambridge University Press, 1997.

McCormick, John P. *Machiavellian Democracy.* Cambridge: Cambridge University Press, 2011.

McCullough, David. *John Adams.* New York: Simon & Schuster, 2001.

Millar, John. *An Historical View of the English Government from the Settlement of the Saxons in Britain, to the Revolution in 1688*. London, 1818.

Mills, C. Wright. *The Power Elite*. Oxford: Oxford University Press, 2000.

Miroff, Bruce. *Icons of Democracy: American Leaders as Heroes, Aristocrats, Dissenters, and Democrats*. Lawrence: University Press of Kansas, 2000.

———. "Merit, Fame, and Political Leadership." *Journal of Politics* 48, no. 1 (1986): 116–32.

Montesquieu. *The Spirit of the Laws*. Translated by Anne M. Cohler, Basia C. Miller, and Harold S. Stone. Cambridge: Cambridge University Press, 1989.

Murray, Charles. *Coming Apart: The State of White America, 1960–2010*. New York: Crown Forum, 2012.

Murrin, John M. "The Legal Transformation: The Bench and Bar of Eighteenth-Century Massachusetts." In *Colonial America: Essays in Politics and Social Development*, edited by Stanley N. Katz, 415–49. Boston: Little, Brown, 1971.

Niebuhr, Reinhold. *The Irony of American History*. Chicago: University of Chicago Press, 2008.

Niles, John Milton. *Speech on the Bill Imposing Additional Duties, as Depositaries in Certain Cases, on Public Officers, &c.* Washington, DC: Globe Office, 1838.

Noble, Marianne. *The Masochistic Pleasures of Sentimental Literature*. Princeton, NJ: Princeton University Press, 2000.

Nye, Joseph S., Jr. *Soft Power: The Means to Success in World Politics*. New York: Public Affairs, 2004.

Paine, Thomas. *Collected Writings*. Edited by Eric Foner. New York: Library of America, 1995.

———. *Rights of Man*. Edited by Gregory Claeys. Indianapolis: Hackett Publishing Company, 1992.

Palmer, R. R. *The Age of the Democratic Revolution: A Political History of Europe and America, 1760–1800*. Princeton, NJ: Princeton University Press, 1970.

Parrington, Vernon Louis. *The Colonial Mind, 1600–1800*. New York, 1927.

Plato. *The Republic of Plato*. Translated by Allan Bloom. New York: Basic Books, 1991.

Pocock, J.G.A. *The Machiavellian Moment: Florentine Political Thought and the Atlantic Republican Tradition*. Princeton, NJ: Princeton University Press, 1975.

Polybius. *The Histories*. Vol. 3, *Books 5–8*. Translated by W. R. Paton. Revised by F. W. Walbank and Christian Habicht. Cambridge, MA: Harvard University Press, 2011.

Proceedings of the Massachusetts Historical Society. 2nd ser. Vol. 17. 1903.

Rakove, Jack N. *Original Meanings: Politics and Ideas in the Making of the Constitution*. New York: Vintage Books, 1996.

Rawls, John. *Political Liberalism*. New York: Columbia University Press, 1996.

Robbins, Caroline. *The Eighteenth-Century Commonwealthman: Studies in the Transmission, Development, and Circumstance of English Liberal Thought from the Restoration of Charles II until the War with the Thirteen Colonies*. Indianapolis: Liberty Fund, 2004.

Rousseau, Jean-Jacques. *Considerations on the Government of Poland and on its Projected Reformation in Rousseau: The Social Contract and Other Political Writings*. Edited and Translated by Victor Gourevitch. Cambridge: Cambridge University Press, 1997.

———. *The Social Contract*. Translated by Maurice Cranston. New York: Penguin Books, 1968.

Sabl, Andrew. *Hume's Politics: Coordination and Crisis in the History of England*. Princeton, NJ: Princeton University Press, 2012.

———. "Noble Infirmity: Love of Fame in Hume." *Political Theory* 34, no. 5 (October 2006): 542–68.

———. *Ruling Passions: Political Offices and Democratic Ethics*. Princeton, NJ: Princeton University Press, 2012.

Sallust. *The War with Catiline*. Translated by J. C. Rolfe. Loeb Classical Library. Cambridge, MA: Harvard University Press, 1921.

Schlozman, Kay Lehman, Sidney Verba, and Henry E. Brady. *The Unheavenly Chorus: Unequal Political Voice and the Broken Promise of American Democracy*. Princeton: Princeton University Press, 2012.

Schutz, John A., and Douglass Adair, eds. *The Spur of Fame: Dialogues of John Adams and Benjamin Rush, 1805–1813*. San Marino, CA: Huntington Library: 1966.

Shklar, Judith N. *Ordinary Vices*. Cambridge, MA: Belknap Press of Harvard University Press, 1984.

———. *Redeeming American Political Thought*. Chicago: University of Chicago Press, 1998.

Smith, Adam. *The Theory of Moral Sentiments*. Edited by D. D. Raphael and A. L. Macfie. Indianapolis: Liberty Fund, 1976.

Smith, Page. *John Adams*. 2 vols. Garden City: Doubleday & Company, 1962.

Staloff, Darren. "John Adams and the Enlightenment." In *A Companion to John Adams and John Quincy Adams*, edited by David Waldstreicher, 36–59. Malden, MA: Wiley-Blackwell, 2013.

Stevens, John. *Observations on Government, Including Some Animadversions on Mr. Adams's Defence of the Constitutions of*

Government of the United States of America: and on Mr. De Lolme's Constitution of England. New York: W. Ross, 1787.

Storing, Herbert J., ed. *The Complete Anti-Federalist.* 7 vols. Chicago: University of Chicago Press, 1981.

———. *What the Anti-Federalists Were* For. Chicago: University of Chicago Press, 1981.

Sunstein, Cass R. "Political Equality and Unintended Consequences." *Columbia Law Review* 94, no. 4 (1994): 1390–1414.

Taylor, John. *An Inquiry into the Principles and Policy of the Government of the United States.* New Haven, CT, 1814.

Thompson, C. Bradley. *John Adams and the Spirit of Liberty.* Lawrence: University Press of Kansas, 1998.

———. "John Adams's Machiavellian Moment." *Review of Politics* 57 (1995): 389–417.

Tocqueville, Alexis De. *Democracy in America.* Edited by Harvey C. Mansfield and Delba Winthrop. Chicago: University of Chicago Press, 2000.

Truman, David B. *The Governmental Process: Political Interests and Public Opinion.* New York: Knopf, 1951.

Vile, M.J.C. *Constitutionalism and the Separation of Powers.* Oxford: Oxford University Press, 1967.

Walzer, Michael. "Liberalism and the Art of Separation." *Political Theory* 12, no. 3 (1984): 315–30.

———. *Spheres of Justice: A Defense of Pluralism and Equality.* New York: Basic Books, 1983.

Weston, Corinne Comstock. *English Constitutional Theory and the House of Lords: 1556–1832.* New York: Columbia University Press, 1965.

Wilentz, Sean. *Rise of American Democracy: Jefferson to Lincoln.* New York: W. W. Norton & Company, 2005.

Winters, Jeffrey. *Oligarchy.* Cambridge: Cambridge University Press, 2012.

Wirls, Daniel, and Stephen Wirls. *The Invention of the United*

States Senate. Baltimore: Johns Hopkins University Press, 2004.

Wolfe, Tom. "The Last American Hero is Junior Johnson. Yes!" *Esquire* (March 1965): 71–74, 138–55.

Wood, Gordon S. *The Creation of the American Republic: 1776–1787*. Chapel Hill: University of North Carolina Press, 1998.

Zuckert, Michael, and Derek A. Webb. *Anti-Federalist Writings of the Melancton Smith Circle*. Edited by Michael Zuckert and Derek A. Webb. Indianapolis: Liberty Fund, 2009.

Index

balanced government (*continued*)
wealth and, 20–22; *Thoughts on
Government* and, 166n38. *See
also* bi-/unicameralism; British
system; divided sovereignty; executive power; mixed constitutions;
ostracism scheme; U.S. Senate
banks, 84, 92, 93, 178n62
beauty, 115–17, 134, 151, 185n48
Berger, Peter, 191n42
"A Bill for the More General Diffusion
of Knowledge" (Jefferson), 69–70
birth, 58–59, 75–76, 80, 81–89, 93, 94,
121, 176n39. *See also* family line-
ages; goods of fortune; wealth
bi-/unicameralism: balanced government and, 28–29, 32, 54; British
model and, 29, 30–31; *Defence*
on, 27, 45, 55–56; French Revolution and, 99–100; oligarchy and,
45, 49–50, 54–56; Stevens's critique
and, 34. *See also* ostracism scheme
Blackstone, William, 163n17
Bodin, Jean, 31
Bolingbroke, 5, 67–68, 179n71
borough system (Britain), 48
Boston Massacre (1770), 6–7
Bowdoin, Madame, 92, 180n82
Brady, Henry E., 160n47
British system, 10, 28, 29, 30–31, 34,
35, 37, 47–48, 163n17. *See also* anti-
court movement; balanced
government
Brooks, David, 117
Burke, Edmund, 10, 121, 139, 163n17

Calhoun, John C., 155n3
Callender, James, 60, 172n5
Calvinism, 171n84
Cassimer, John, 52
*The Changing Political Thought of John
Adams* (Howe), 148
character, 59, 64, 101, 142. *See also* virtue

Charles I (Britain), 163n17
Charles VII (France), 47
Charondas, 90
Cicero, 5
classes, socio-economic (estates/orders/
ranks): American exceptionalism
and, 150; Anti-Federalists/Federal-
ists and, 23–27; balanced government and, 31–32, 34; Machiavelli
on, 43–44, 169n60; New England
and, 7; republicanism and, 9, 10,
157n23; Rome and, 47; Tocqueville
on, 150–51; virtue and, 79. *See also*
aristocracy; representation; wealth
commercial societies: distinctions of
wealth and, 143–44; honors and,
146–47; power of elite and, 46; soft
power and, 122–23; sympathy for
rich and, 106, 114, 138, 140, 143–44;
titles and, 125–26, 133–34. *See also*
avarice (greed); speculation
Commonwealth of Oceana (Harrington), 70–71, 81
commonwealths, 164n23
Complete Anti-Federalist (M. Smith),
161n8
Condorcet, Nicolas de, 30, 34, 165n32
conscience, 112–13. *See also* morality
conservatism, 10. *See also* Anglomanes
*Considerations on the Government in
Poland* (Rousseau), 124, 140–41,
177n47
Constituent Assembly of 1789 (France),
30–31, 34
The Constitution of England (De Lolme),
31, 37–40, 168n43
Continental Congress, 61
Creation of the American Republic
(Wood), 12, 178n57
credit, 84–85

Dahl, Robert, 96
Davila, Enrico Caterino, 100

political science, 5, 11, 13, 14, 18, 149
Politics (Aristotle), 79–80
Polybius, 29–30, 163n17, 166n38
the poor: creditors and, 84–85; desire
    for distinction and, 107, 111, 113,
    136; education and, 7, 71; material
    dependency and, 74–75, 111; as pre-
    rich, 118; as Roman Consuls, 141;
    sympathy for, 101, 114; sympathy
    for rich and, 102; U.S. Constitu-
    tion and, 25, 26. *See also* the disem-
    powered; equality/inequality;
    laboring classes; oppression
Pope, Alexander, 100
popular assemblies. *See* bi-/unicamer-
    alism; majorities; representation;
    U.S. Senate
popular sovereignty, 27, 37, 40–41,
    64–66, 81, 82–83, 169n57, 171n94.
    See also Rousseau, Jean-Jacques
populism, 13
poverty. *See* the poor
The Power Elite (Mills), 9
power (influence) of elites: Anti-
    Federalists on, 23–27, 65, 162n8;
    beauty and, 115–17; *Defence* on, 6,
    27, 45, 55–56, 72–81, 87–88; formal
    (legal), 9, 24, 50–51, 56, 58, 59,
    62–63, 80; goods of fortune and,
    93; New England and, 7, 73; pop-
    ular sovereignty and, 27; purchase
    of, 14, 15, 17–18, 97, 122, 182n6; right
    to, 98; soft, 122–23; withdrawal
    from public life and, 118–19, 181n1.
    See also aristocracy; balanced gov-
    ernment; family lineages; goods
    of fortune; oligarchy; oppression;
    ostracism scheme; wealth
praise. *See* distinction and praise
presidency. *See* executive power
Price, Richard, 99–100
priestly class, 7, 83
privileges, legal (formal), 9, 24, 50–51,
    56, 58, 59, 62–63

progressivism, 12
property, 6, 77, 83, 140, 161n8, 180n1,
    191n6
psychology, moral, 14, 16, 18, 97–101,
    122, 149, 181n17. *See also* beauty;
    distinction and praise; human
    nature; sympathy/admiration for
    the rich
public good (public interest), 45–46,
    135–36, 137, 158n27, 179n71, 187n18,
    191n26. *See also* commonwealth
public opinion, 14, 18, 72, 97, 159n36.
    See also sympathy/admiration for
    the rich
Pulteney, William, 36

Rakove, Jack N., 170n71
Rawls, John, 17
reactionary interpretations, 12, 32
reason, 112–13, 137, 171n84
rebellions, 40, 47
Reflections on the Revolution in France
    (Burke), 139
religion, 10, 138, 182n13, 191n6
representation, 23, 32, 37, 45–52, 54,
    65, 90, 170n71. *See also* balanced
    government; bi-/unicameralism;
    elections; meritocracy; popular
    sovereignty
Republic (Plato), 71, 74, 97–98
republicanism: Adams and, 1–2, 3–4,
    4–5, 11, 155n8; balanced govern-
    ment *versus*, 29, 31–32; classes and,
    10, 157n23; defined, 45; distinction
    and, 185n30, 190n21; education
    and, 91; meritocracy and, 62–65,
    70–71; popular derivation of of-
    fices and, 165n26; power of elites
    and, 149; 17th century influences,
    177n55; *Thoughts on Government*
    and, 3; titles and dignities and, 126,
    128–29, 131–32, 142
republics: ambition and, 136; aristoc-
    racy and, 24, 42; democracies